SOMETHING OLD, SOMETHING NEW

SOMETHING OLD, SOMETHING NEW

Contemporary Entanglements of
Religion and Secularity

Wayne Glausser

*To Brother Raphael,
my first real
teacher.
Wayne Glausser*

OXFORD
UNIVERSITY PRESS

Oxford University Press is a department of the University of Oxford. It furthers
the University's objective of excellence in research, scholarship, and education
by publishing worldwide. Oxford is a registered trade mark of Oxford University
Press in the UK and certain other countries.

Published in the United States of America by Oxford University Press
198 Madison Avenue, New York, NY 10016, United States of America.

CIP data is on file at the Library of Congress
ISBN 978-0-19-086417-0

1 3 5 7 9 8 6 4 2
Printed by Sheridan Books, Inc., United States of America

For Marnie, now and forever

CONTENTS

CONTENTS

PREFACE

This will be an untraditional preface. More a postscript than a preface, and in some sense supererogatory, it is certainly not something I had planned to include as part of the book. I decided, however, that under the circumstances I could not keep it out.

As I was writing *Something Old, Something New: Contemporary Entanglements of Religion and Secularity,* my own life became entangled with its subject matter in a startling way. I had drafted most of the chapter on "Psychedelic Last Rites"—the book's final chapter as things now stand, but chronologically the third piece I undertook. This chapter compares the traditional Catholic sacrament of extreme unction with recent experiments in which scientists give psychedelic drugs to terminal cancer patients. In both the old sacrament and the new experiments, the goal is to help dying people find peace as they manage their last days. By fortifying souls, or reorienting consciousness, priests and psychiatrists hope to alleviate depression by giving the dying a fresh perspective on life, death, and the universe.

Literally middraft—sitting at a table in the university library, composing my analysis of the most recent clinical trials—I received a call from my doctor: much to his surprise, he said, a biopsy revealed that I have metastatic cancer of an incurable sort. Treatments might stall the cancer's progress for a while, but my diagnosis was unmistakably terminal.

The synchronicity of the moment struck with such force that it felt surreal. After a few days of numbness and disorientation, I decided that fate had presented me with an unusual challenge. I had joined the ranks of dying penitents and clinical subjects; I was no longer safely outside the experience I was writing about. Could this piece of writing I had drafted do me any good, as I stood at the cosmic threshold that only a few days before had seemed a benign abstraction?

My chapter compared two more or less sacramental means of sorting things out. If I had wanted to try either one, this would have proved difficult. I did not have the faith required for extreme unction. I was raised Catholic by my mother, but switched over to my father's atheism during my teens; in my more mature reflective life, I have found myself attracted to (and repelled by) elements of both. I probably would have qualified for a psychedelic experiment, but those trials had closed to volunteers, and besides, I did not feel as if I needed a latter-day entheogenic boost. I had already undertaken my psychedelic trials in college adventures with LSD and other drugs of that sort. There were no psychiatrists to guide the trips—this was strictly do-it-yourself—but my memories of those experiences remain among my most vivid. As I tapped back into them, and compared my memories with the reports of subjects who took LSD or psilocybin in clinical settings, I found that my psychedelic experience proved very helpful as existential fortification.

I would prefer not to go into detail about my do-it-yourself psychedelic therapy: partly to keep from straying too far off course, partly because psychedelic profundities never translate very well onto the page. I will just say that my memories of psychedelic consciousness contributed substantially to equanimity in the face of death. Other things mattered even more, at least for me; and I am not confident that either psychedelic therapy or Catholic last rites will sufficiently fortify spirits in the absence of loving family and friends.

After my diagnosis, I wrote and revised this book with a greater sense of urgency. The last chapter obviously mattered in a new way. Writing the chapter on deadly sins, I found unexpected relevance in the sin of sloth. The darkest form of sloth, acedia, poses an insidious threat to the terminally ill. I also found myself newly sensitized to pride, the best camouflaged of the deadly sins. I have no doubt that pride contributes in its usual secret ways to anxiety about death. I read back through "The Rhetoric of New Atheism" to make sure I was satisfied with its approach to why the world exists. This is a question that has always intrigued me, and now it seemed especially important to have the best available bottom-line concepts—not only to pass along good information, but as part of my existential fortification. As I drafted "The Rhetoric of Faithful Science," my new situation catalyzed doubts about certain elements of the scientists' apologetics, most notably in the matter of cancerous "glitches" in God's language of DNA. I also took special interest in tracking down the religious positions of Einstein and Spinoza, his spiritual mentor. The more I looked into their reflections, the more I found that their hard-to-label beliefs best coincided with my own. I have never been comfortable calling myself a theist, an atheist, or an agnostic. Pressed for a label, as I might be over these last however many months, I will say, "I'm a Spinozist. A Romantic Spinozist."

I am more than ready to bring this preface to a close and let the book speak for itself. I hope that it will turn out to be as thought-provoking for others—whatever their beliefs, however they manage their entanglements of religion and secularity—as it has been for me.

ACKNOWLEDGMENTS

I am grateful to many students and colleagues over the last few years who have helped me shape the ideas in this book. In particular, I would like to thank Jeffrey Kenney, who generously shared his expertise in matters of religious studies; Keith Nightenhelser, classicist and polymath, who offered suggestions about a number of subjects; and Michael Sinowitz, equal parts skeptic and enthusiast, who inspired this project more than he probably realizes with good wine and conversation. DePauw University granted a sabbatical leave that gave me the time and resources to write.

I was fortunate to have the support of Cynthia Read of Oxford University Press, who led the way in bringing this project to fruition. Suggestions offered by readers in the review process helped me clarify and augment some theoretical elements.

I thank my doctors at Indiana University Health, for obvious and not-so-obvious reasons: some of them seemed genuinely interested in what I was writing, and no doubt kept other patients waiting as we discussed this or that chapter.

And as I imply in the preface, I could not have managed this part of my life without the love that flowed, every day, from Annie, Meg, and Marnie. I will not even attempt to express how much they mean to me, and how lucky I feel when I am around them.

Chapter 1

Entanglement

An Introduction (with Starbucks Cups and Stem Cells)

I have chosen the word "entanglement" to describe the relationship between religion and secularity that most interests me and provides the foundation for this book. Entanglement as I would define it differs from four other common configurations of that relationship. After offering a brief definition of entanglement and contrasting it with the other four models, I use this introduction to flesh out entanglement with two examples. One example comes from the "War on Christmas," the term used by Christian traditionalists to criticize the secularist degradation of their holiday; the other comes from controversies surrounding embryonic stem cell research. In both of these examples, and in the six more extensive analyses that follow, something old from religious tradition becomes entangled with something new from contemporary secularity.

The term "secularity" is probably understood by most readers in its familiar senses, which are congruent with its historical origins—that is to say, some degree of resistance to religion, adherence to materialism and the scientific method, and a focus on life in this world rather than any afterlife or transcendent purpose. Recent scholarship in religious studies, however, has subjected this traditional concept of secularity to re-examination and rendered it more problematic. Later in the introduction, I review how these new scholarly descriptions of secularity compare with the more common understanding of the term, and how they align with my notion of entangled religion and secularity.

My concept of entanglement refers to a contentious but oddly intimate relationship between religion and secularity. Secular ideas compete with corresponding religious convictions, but in entanglement, neither side simply dominates by displacing the other. As traditional religious knowledge and values come into conflict with their secular counterparts, the old ideas undergo stress and adaptation, but the influence works in both directions. Those with primary allegiance to secular interests find themselves entangled with aspects of religious thinking that cannot be dismissed as silly or irrelevant. Whether they do it intentionally or without knowing, entangled secularists engage with and sometimes borrow from an older mode of thinking they believe they have surpassed. Religious and secular interests are entangled in three senses of the word. Entangled can mean "involved in mental difficulties, perplexed, bewildered," as well as "interlaced in such a manner that a separation cannot easily be made" (*OED*). Mental difficulties abound in the entanglements I discuss, and religious values interlace sufficiently with secularity to prevent an easy separation of one from the other. A third useful meaning comes from modern physics, with the puzzling phenomenon known as quantum entanglement. Two apparently separate particles, at quite some distance from each other, actually behave as if they were linked: what we observe or measure in one particle will determine the state of the other. Entangled religion and secularity share something of this quantum model—however distant from each other they might seem, or however convenient it might be for one to shed the other once and for all.

FOUR OTHER MODELS

Entanglement differs, of course, from the poisonously simple animosity between religious and secular interests that catalyzes crises of violence. My focus lies elsewhere, with four versions of nonentanglement that manifest not as crisis but as normal cultural conversation. In each one, an interpretive community holding certain assumptions manages to circumvent any significant entanglement of religion and secularity. In three of these four configurations, secularity refers mainly to materialism, scientific method, and the body of knowledge thereby derived. Debates about religion and science figure prominently in this book and many others, to be sure; but secularity means more than just science. It also suggests broader cultural associations with pluralism, toleration, and liberal political interests.

In the first nonentanglement model, religion and secularity keep separate because conservative believers dismiss secular science rather than engage creditably with it. A good example drawn from Christian communities would be the Young Earth Creationists. Their numbers are hard to estimate, but they probably have more influence than secular scientists would like to believe. The "Creation Museum," a theme park in Kentucky dedicated to Young Earth ideas, remains a popular attraction. One prominent spokesperson for the Young Earth view is Dr. Terry Mortenson, whose manifesto has been widely distributed as a teaching tool.[1] Christians who believe in Young Earth Creationism insist that "Genesis is history, not poetry, parable, prophetic vision, or mythology." They take the six days of creation narrated in Genesis to mean "six literal (24-hour) days, which occurred 6,000–12,000 years ago." In order to counteract the abundant scientific evidence for a much older earth and the evolution of species over hundreds of millions of years, Young Earthers depend on the Biblical account of Noah's flood (which they believe happened some four to five thousand years ago). Noah, they say, did not manage to gather pairs of all animals then living on earth: "All land animals and birds not in Noah's Ark (along with many sea creatures) perished, many of which were subsequently buried in the Flood sediments." Hence the evidence for so many extinct species, including dinosaurs, that literally missed the boat.

Young Earth Creationists are aware of modern geology and biology, which they attribute to "godless men (scientists who rejected the Bible as God's inerrant Word)." But their absolute adherence to biblical literalism prevents them from meaningfully engaging (and entangling) with secular science. Their argument against the Big Bang has nothing to do with Hubble, Father Lemaitre, Penzias and Wilson, or Hawking. "The Bible says the Earth was created before the sun and the stars," they remind us: hence the Big Bang theory cannot be right. Many of their arguments flatly deny evidence for evolution. Evolution claims that birds evolved from dinosaurs, but this must be wrong, because Genesis says that "birds were created before the dinosaurs (which were made on Day 6, since they are land animals)." Their rejection of evolution goes all the way down to the origin of species. "God created the first animate and inanimate things supernaturally and instantly," they say, which means that all animals came into being "fully formed and fully functioning. For example, plants, animals, and people were mature adults ready to reproduce naturally 'after their kinds.'" Young Earth Creationists and other believers who resemble them, from whatever faith, do not find themselves entangled with science. They push science aside to make room for their religious convictions. Some secularists conversely push aside religion to clear the ground for atheism. Not all of the writers who might be called "new atheists" treat religious beliefs as ridiculous, twisted fantasies, but some of them do, including the influential voices of Richard Dawkins and Christopher Hitchens. Dawkins and Hitchens set themselves above religious beliefs of all sorts and produce secularist manifestos. The titles alone of two of their books make their disdain clear enough: Dawkins's *The God Delusion* and Hitchens's *God Is Not Great: How Religion Poisons Everything*. A couple of snippets from the latter will suffice to represent the secular dismissal of religion. Religion in all its forms, Hitchens says, emerged at a time when no humans "had the smallest idea of what was going on. It comes from the bawling and fearful infancy of our species and is a babyish attempt to meet our inescapable demand for knowledge."[2] As for the Bible, it "was put together by crude, uncultured human mammals" and should be chucked aside as a toxic influence.[3] Here is the exact converse of the Young Earthers' literalist devotion to scripture. For them, everything in the Bible is sacred and indisputable; for Hitchens, everything in it is primitive, worthless nonsense.

Although I argue in chapter 2 that, in significant ways, the writings of new atheists do entangle with the religious ideas they hope to supplant, there is no discernible entanglement in much of Hitchens's and Dawkins's work. They pay as little respect to religious ideas as the Young Earthers did to geology and evolution. Bill Maher's film *Religulous* similarly holds religion up for ridicule; he sets up meetings with a variety of religious figures whose ideas are plainly ludicrous from a secular perspective. If Maher had instead been interested in finding entanglement, he had at least one good opportunity to do so. Outside the Vatican, he bumps into Father

Reginald Foster, who surprises Maher with his unorthodox views. Foster debunks Christmas rituals as silly—they are based on "nice stories" that are not true. He also shrugs off the idea of hell and eternal punishment: "That's the old Catholic thing. . . . That's all gone."[4] Maher might have shifted gears here and pursued entanglement instead of ridicule. What did the priest mean about hell? What does a "new" Catholic think about the afterlife and the nature of salvation? Why does Foster even remain a priest? The discussion might have proven quite thought-provoking for Maher, who was raised with traditional ideas of hell. Apparently Maher has not read around in recent Catholic debates about the subject, but Father Foster might have given him new ideas. One Catholic theologian, for example, has proposed an interesting analogy: hell may be something like the empty feeling of missing a good party, rather than the experience of overt, painful punishments.[5] Perhaps Maher would find himself revising his simple condemnation of Catholicism. But that is not the film he wanted to make. He cuts away from the complicated priest to a new example of religious silliness.

In a third version of nonentanglement, religious thinking and scientific thinking sit apart from each other as equally dignified but essentially distinct modes of inquiry. Religion and science pose fundamentally different questions about the world; each provides answers that the other cannot, and we need both of them. Although there have certainly been times when religion and science competed for dominance, a more mature view is to treat them as complementary allies. Stephen Jay Gould most influentially theorized this model and gave it a name: NOMA, for Non-Overlapping Magisteria. Gould defines the magisterium of science as "a teaching authority dedicated to using the mental methods and observational techniques validated by success and experience as particularly well suited for describing, and attempting to explain, the factual construction of nature."[6] The complementary magisterium of religion engages in questions of ethics and meaning rather than natural facts. This magisterium also "includes several disciplines traditionally grouped under the humanities—much of philosophy, and part of literature and history"; with this clarification, Gould includes even atheists and agnostics as participants in "religious" thinking.[7] Gould illustrates NOMA with the example of inquiry into human relationships with other organisms. Science gives us plenty of information about things like percentages of shared DNA, evolutionary adaptations and branchings, and causes of extinction. Religion "raises a host of questions with an entirely different thrust: Are we worth more than bugs or bacteria because we have evolved a much more complex neurology? Under what conditions (if ever) do we have a right to drive other species to extinction by elimination of their habitats?"[8] Framed this way, Gould's NOMA sounds sensible enough. Many people find it the most convenient way to theorize religion and science. But neither the new atheists of chapter 2 nor the faithful scientists of chapter 3 find NOMA a compelling model. For them, there is simply too much overlap between the two magisteria to keep them separate. As scientists discover more facts about the neurological complexity of bugs, to use Gould's example, we may well revise our ethical ideas about how humans ought to interact with them. When Catholics examine possible miracles as they vet candidates for sainthood, they consult scientists and use scientific methods. Many believers viewed scientific evidence of the Big Bang as confirmation of divine revelation about the origin of the universe. NOMA declares a comfortable truce between religion and science, but it sweeps under the rug too many occasions of significant overlap.

A final version of nonentanglement connects with the broader sense of secularity—that is, not just science and its methods, but a set of cultural values that may seem at odds with those of many traditional religions. In this model, religion and secularity overlap with and contradict one another, but the two are allowed to coexist in a First-Amendment-friendly détente. I like to call this the "thoughts and prayers" model of nonentanglement; it reflects current American culture, which is in principle democratic and tolerant, but remains predominately religious. The phrase "thoughts and prayers" registers even-handedly both secular and religious perspectives.

"Thoughts and prayers" has become one of the more successful memes in popular rhetoric. Whenever a political leader delivers a speech expressing sympathy after a tragedy, he or she *always* sends "thoughts and prayers" to those affected. (There may be exceptions, but I cannot recall one.) When friends send messages of comfort to someone in distress—someone, say, who has just received a cancer diagnosis—they will likely use the same cliché. This expression conveniently joins but separates the "prayers" of the religious from the "thoughts" that represent secular acts of sympathy. This handy rhetorical device prevents any cultural divisiveness from intruding on a heartfelt message. A religious person receiving the message will welcome the prayers of a fellow believer; a secular person will appreciate the thoughts, and tolerate the prayers. "Thoughts and prayers" has succeeded as a meme because it carries out its purpose effectively, if blandly. It yokes together the religious and secular worlds all the while keeping them distinct. It placates both audiences. The success of the cliché comes with a price, however. Everyone receives it as an obligatory formula; no one is either offended or particularly moved by it. Just as real estate agents recognize about an interior room painted off-white, no one is likely to react badly to it, even if no one has much enthusiasm for it.

HAPPY HOLIDAYS

Things become much more animated and interesting when strategies of separation give way to entanglement. As a first example of entanglement, it might be helpful to look at another bland meme that aims, like "thoughts and prayers," for inoffensive inclusion of both religious and secular perspectives: "happy holidays." This phrase has led not to harmony but to vivid cultural conflict. For over a decade now, religious conservatives have referred to this conflict as the secularist "War on Christmas." The substitution of "happy holidays" for "Merry Christmas" in public discourse—especially in political and commercial contexts—became their first and most inflammatory cause.

One reason "happy holidays" leads to entanglement, whereas "thoughts and prayers" does not, has to do with a rhetorical difference between the two memes. "Thoughts and prayers" keeps religion and secularity safely partitioned with its paratactic structure: the two nouns thereby take on separate but equal status. The same rhetorical strategy would not work well for "happy holidays." Any paratactic list would prove unwieldy, as in "Merry Christmas and Hanukkah and Kwanzaa and Yule," and so forth. "Happy holidays" instead delivers a type of metonymy in which a whole stands for a part. (A couple of other popular examples of whole-for-part metonymy: aisles that use the heading "feminine products" for tampons; and when airline pilots say, "We have some weather ahead," where "weather" means a thunderstorm.) The word "holidays" includes any number of such occasions clustered around the winter solstice. As a rhetorical device, whole-for-part metonymy often serves the purposes of euphemism (see both examples in parentheses above). "Happy holidays" does carry something of a euphemistic effect, because it allows a speaker to avoid naming something specific that is potentially offensive. But "happy holidays" stirs up trouble instead of quieting it. Meant to be inoffensively inclusive, it offends everyone for whom "Merry Christmas" seems the natural, essential expression. "Happy holidays" swallows "Merry Christmas" instead of linking up with it.

This would-be euphemism recently upset the likes of Sarah Palin, Pat Buchanan, and Bill O'Reilly, but their resentment has precedents well back in American history. Early in the twentieth century, anti-Semitic articles appearing in Henry Ford's newsweeklies blamed Jewish influence for the suppression of "Merry Christmas."[9] In the 1950s, the anticommunist John Birch Society saw the rise of "holiday" references as a sign of eroding patriotism, masterminded by godless Soviets.[10] Fox host O'Reilly introduced the contemporary conflict in 2004 under the headline "Christmas under Siege." O'Reilly blamed not Jews or communists but "secularists": "If the secularists can destroy religion in the public arena, the brave new progressive world is a possibility. That's what happened in Canada."[11] His coinage of "The War on Christmas" stuck as the label for secularist aggression.

The warriors defending Christmas have attempted to change the "holiday" culture of corporations with threats of boycott. The American Family Association tracks commercial messaging and judges corporations to be "for Christmas," "marginal on Christmas," or "against Christmas."[12] Many "marginal" or "against" corporations had adopted the inclusive "holiday" phrasing to avoid offending potential customers. For them, no doubt, it amounted to a marketing calculation rather than a principled stand on democracy and theocracy. "Merry Christmas" advocates were simply trying to change the math. In using boycott as a strategy, however, these conservative traditionalists showed their entanglement with secular interests. They tacitly acknowledged that Christmas had become a secular economic event of great consequence, not simply—or even primarily—a religious celebration. Corporations depend on the accelerated commerce of the Christmas season to make their enterprises profitable. Warriors for Christmas would never say so, but their threats of boycott confirm a secular viewpoint: Jesus is not the *only* reason for the season.

The corporation that stirred up the most controversy was Starbucks. A report surfaced that baristas had been instructed not to greet customers with "Merry Christmas." (Starbucks has denied ever giving such instructions.) Then came the affair of the holiday cups. Each year in December, they issue a new cup with a design to mark the season. In 2015, the new cup infuriated the defenders of Christmas: it was a plain red design, with no images suggestive of Christmas. Conservative pastor Joshua Feuerstein used social media to condemn Starbucks: they had erased all signs of Christmas from their cups, he claimed, "because they hate Jesus."[13] Feuerstein's zeal went viral.

Starbucks had never actually depicted Jesus on its cups, or any other explicitly religious image; earlier years had used reindeer, tree ornaments, and the like. American courts have consistently ruled that images of Santa, reindeer, and trees, while associated with Christmas, should be regarded as secular symbols. (The issue comes up in First Amendment cases about the use of public spaces.) For Feuerstein and his supporters, this made no difference. Their (unarticulated) logic apparently goes something like this. Santa's reindeer and tree ornaments are semiological markers that represent only one holiday, Christmas; Christmas is in its essence a Christian celebration of the birth of Jesus; therefore, the deletion of Santa, reindeer, and similar images amounts to a rejection of Jesus. The argument has flaws, to be sure—it ignores the non-Christian roots of much

Christmas imagery—but it is not on the face of it absurd. Courts may well call Santa a secular symbol, but his name means "saint," the nickname "Kris Kringle" derives from the German *Christkind*, and he judges people's naughty or nice behavior as a sort of surrogate for the Christian deity. Santa presents a knotty entanglement of religious and secular referents.

It may seem that the Starbucks controversy and the War on Christmas are trivial matters, hardly worth the trouble for either side. But you never know. Eric Trump, son of Donald, said that his father decided to run for president after he heard that the White House now referred to its "holiday tree."[14] (President Obama actually had a "Christmas tree" throughout his tenure; Trump may have been thinking of a similar controversy involving the Capitol tree, which went by "holiday tree" for the first few years of this century.) During his campaign, he took note of the plain red cups and said, "Maybe we should boycott Starbucks. I don't know." He added, "If I become president, we're gonna be saying 'Merry Christmas' at every store. You can leave 'Happy Holidays' at the corner."[15]

STEM CELLS

The new president may have to weigh in on another entanglement of religion and secularity, this one connected to science and with much higher stakes: embryonic stem cell research. Both of his predecessors made decisions that had important consequences for scientists. President Bush greatly restricted the number of stem cells that would be made available for federally funded research. President Obama reversed course and substantially increased access to them. Advocates of stem cell research argue that this approach will prove extremely helpful in treating serious illnesses and injuries, including

Alzheimer's, Parkinson's, juvenile diabetes, and spinal cord damage; stem cell research might also lead to new treatments for cancer. Critics counter that using and thereby destroying a human embryo, even for these purposes, violates basic moral standards.

In 1998, James Thomson of the University of Wisconsin-Madison successfully isolated and removed stem cells from human embryos that had been donated by fertility clinics. Fertility clinics hold in storage many thousands of embryos that are left over and no longer needed after a successful in vitro pregnancy. (An initial extraction of some fifteen eggs is considered the most effective way to achieve a good result; all the eggs are fertilized and become embryos, but only one or a few that look most promising are implanted.) Thomson and his successors use these leftover embryos to harvest pluripotent stem cells, which have the potential to become any type of cell in the body. Thomson and another group from Tokyo later reported promising results in creating pluripotent stem cells from adult skin, which would circumvent the moral difficulties surrounding the use of embryos. But scientists, including Thomson, are not at all sure that these adult cells would ever prove as effective as embryonic cells for therapeutic breakthroughs.

Debates over embryonic stem cells show entanglement at work in full complexity. Four different voices carry authority in these debates. Scientists like Thomson have spoken about their work; all the major religions have articulated official positions; bioethicists have applied their philosophical methods; and perhaps most significantly, political leaders have had to justify their decisions and votes. With all four types of authority, religious as well as scientific perspectives come into play. Both science and religion make compelling claims that cannot be ignored.

The entanglement is least obvious, as one would expect, in statements by scientists who do stem cell research. Consider the following remarks by James Thomson, the Wisconsin researcher who first harvested an embryonic stem cell. He was asked by an interviewer about the moral implications of his work: "The bottom line is that there are 400,000 frozen embryos in the United States, and a large percentage of those are going to be thrown out. Regardless of what you think the moral status of those embryos is, it makes sense to me that it's a better moral decision to use them to help people than just to throw them out. It's a very complex issue, but to me it boils down to that one thing."[16] When Thomson concedes that "it's a very complex issue," he means the moral questions anyone faces when they have to decide whether to throw out and destroy a superfluous embryo. Thomson's confident conclusion only works because he evades the underlying moral questions. Other parties, presumably the parents, have made the decision to discard unneeded embryos; the scientist is presented with a fait accompli. Thomson acknowledges the importance of moral perspectives that are entangled with the science—that make the situation "complex"—but in practice he need not worry about them.

Statements issued by the major churches are meant to guide their respective congregations, but someone viewing them all from a distance would find little help. Their moral conclusions do not point toward any consensus.[17] Catholics and some Protestant churches—Lutherans, Southern Baptists, and Evangelicals—absolutely oppose any destruction of human embryos to harvest stem cells. For them, life begins at the moment of fertilization, and there can be no compromise. Religious truth trumps any rationale secular science can offer. Several other religions approve the harvesting of stem cells for therapeutic purposes, provided the embryos would otherwise have been thrown out. Their moral reasoning, in other words, conforms to the logic of science as articulated by Thomson. This position is held by Jews, Episcopalians, Presbyterians, Unitarians, and

Methodists. Two of the world's largest religions, Buddhism and Islam, do not take a definite stance on this question. For Buddhists, the stem cell situation pits two of their moral principles against each other: a prohibition on doing harm to human life, and a fundamental obligation to alleviate suffering whenever possible. Islam has not reached a consensus as to when organic matter can be said to have a soul; some align with the Catholic position, while others believe the earliest fertilized material has not yet become a human life. The National Council of Churches, an interdenominational group, declines to take a position on the use of embryonic stem cells, because they find no consensus among scientists and ethicists.

One academic bioethicist, Laurie Zoloth of Northwestern, has been an influential voice in that community. In 2004, the US Senate invited Zoloth to give expert testimony on the stem cell controversies. She emphatically endorsed embryonic stem cell research, but in the process of arguing her position, she showed senators a fine example of the entanglement of religion and secularity. She began by acknowledging that religious faith is the primary determinant of anyone's ethical stance in this matter. "I think we cannot come to some sort of agreement on what most divides us today—when human life begins," she told the senators, "for this is a profoundly religious question in a profoundly religious country, profoundly dedicated to the proposition that our freedom to faithfully interpret our faith is the core of American life."[18] She continued with a description of her personal faith and how it has shaped her position on the core issue: "As an orthodox Jew, I understand" that an embryo in its blastocyst stage "is far before our tradition considers it a human person. . . . While I understand the passion and the conviction of those for whom the blastocyst is a person from the moment of fertilization, I do not believe this, and it is a matter of faith for me as well."[19]

Zoloth emphatically described her position on embryonic life as a matter of faith. But at the same time she wove into her testimony a strong suggestion that her position—and only her position—has scientific validity. Even as she explained that any such conviction depends strictly on religious faith, she stealthily brought science to bear on behalf of her particular faith tradition. In the quotation that begins "As an orthodox Jew" and ends with "it is a matter of faith for me as well," the middle section (elided above) posits something like a scientific claim about what a blastocyst really is: "I understand the blastocyst, made in the lab, at the very first stages of division, prior to the time it could even successfully be transferred to a woman's body, as just what it is at that moment: a cluster of primitive cells."[20] Zoloth momentarily veered away from "matter of faith" to matters of scientific fact—she claimed to know the blastocyst as "just what it is." The scientific facts as she shaped them are open to dispute. "Blastocyst" (from the Greek word *blastos* for "sprout") refers to an embryo about five days along with cells that have divided into two types. Zoloth's use of the phrase "primitive cells" tips the argument her way, but "primitive" has no clear scientific meaning here. Her assertion that a blastocyst is not ready for transfer to a womb is vulnerable to challenge: fertility clinics often implant at the blastocyst stage with success. This is not to say that Zoloth's scientific claims are simply mistaken. Scientists refer to the blastocyst as a precursor to the fetus, and in this sense a blastocyst might be called primitive. But no scientific distinctions can indisputably draw a dividing line between the sprout and the mature organism it will become. Zoloth knows this—which is why she began and ended with appeals to faith.

One of the senators whom Zoloth addressed had particular interest in the stem cell controversy. Bill Frist of Tennessee, a heart transplant surgeon before he became Senate majority leader, later delivered a speech on the subject to his colleagues. One senator afterwards called it the most important Senate speech in years. The bottom line is that Frist had decided to support federal funding of embryonic stem cell research. His position surprised many, because Frist, a devout Christian, ardently opposes abortion. His speech on the floor of the Senate presents another good example of entanglement.

Frist began by juxtaposing his pro-life religious position with his scientific perspective on the promise of stem cell research: "Right now, to derive embryonic stem cells, an embryo—which many, including myself, consider nascent human life—must be destroyed. But I also strongly believe—as do countless other scientists, clinicians, and doctors—that embryonic stem cells uniquely hold specific promise for some therapies and potential cures that adult stem cells cannot provide."[21] Frist used the phrase "nascent human life" in contrast with Zoloth's "cluster of primitive cells." Rhetorically at least, the senator remained steadfast in his pro life position. But he countered with another rhetorical move: he prefaced the scientific view with "I strongly believe," borrowing the language of faith to convey a scientific conviction. Frist entangled religion and science because he could not simply grant precedence to one over the other.

Just after he declared he will vote in favor of federal funding, he explained his decision in another entangled passage. He first affirmed his religious convictions: "I am pro-life. I believe human life begins at conception. It is at this moment that an organism is complete—yes, immature—but complete. . . . And it is biologically human. It is living. This position is consistent with my faith." Frist then pivoted toward science, saying, "But to me, it isn't just a matter of faith. It is a fact of science."[22] This move proved crucial to his argument. He knew, given the religious diversity of the Senate (and the country), he could not persuade simply on the basis of faith.

At this point in the speech, at least from Frist's perspective, science and faith agree: the "fact of science" to which he referred is that an embryo is human. He thereafter relied on science to steer the argument away from pro-life orthodoxy. The therapeutic potential of stem cell research, which he described in precise medical detail, allowed him to view such research as itself pro-life—even if its implementation will violate a basic tenet of pro-life conviction.

Frist faces this difficulty candidly. He asks, "So how do we reconcile these differing views?" He answers not with reconciliation, but a suggestion that some form of entanglement may be inevitable: "As individuals, each of us holds views shaped by factors of intellect, of emotion, of spirit."[23] For this thoughtful senator, intellect needs spirit and spirit needs intellect. Frist both adheres to something old—a traditional belief about the human soul—and argues for something new, a promising technology of cell manipulation and the utilitarian logic that justifies its use.

SECULARITY RECONSIDERED

In a contemporary world where secular interests clash conspicuously with religious values—in specific controversies such as stem cell research, and more generally in the inflamed global politics of the twenty-first century—religious studies scholars have been engaged in re-examining the meanings of the term "secularity." As one would expect, this academic attention has led to considerable complication of the ordinary uses of this term as deployed outside of religious studies scholarship. A number of scholars influenced by Michel Foucault have constructed genealogies of secularism that challenge traditional intellectual histories relevant to its rise in the Western world. These traditional histories and meanings have not died out, to be sure, even within scholarly conversation. But the new meanings of secularity have enriched this critical term and will help to situate the entanglements that are the subject of this book.

The term "secularism" has its origins in the work of George Jacob Holyoake, an English writer and social reformer from the middle of the nineteenth century. Holyoake, commonly labeled a "free-thinker," eventually found himself convicted of blasphemy in a society still not secular enough to do away with such laws. According to Holyoake, secularism consisted of three essential principles, which he expressed as follows: "The improvement of this life by material means; that science is the available Providence of Man; that it is good to do good. Whether there be other good or not, the good of the present life is good, and it is good to seek that good."[24] Although Holyoake hedges a little about "whether there be other good or not" (that is, whether there might exist a transcendent good beyond the reach of scientific reasoning), he clearly understands human purpose as the use of science to improve lives in this material world. His original definition of secularism remains, for the most part, consistent with the term as it enters contemporary public conversation. The constituent principles of secularity include materialism, scientific method, liberal reform, and marginalization or rejection of religious transcendence. England and other modern states eventually acknowledged the influence of secularity by institutionalizing toleration and separating church from state.

Given what might be called this classic or public definition of secularity, secularity becomes either a threat to soul and society (for those who believe in the truths contained in revelation and religious doctrine), or a liberating power that will help humans shed the pernicious effects of religious illusion. Many churches have warned of the corrupting influence of secular humanism, especially as academic institutions increasingly come to be dominated by secular voices. On the other side, the work of the most strident new atheists pits secular virtue against religious faith in stark binary opposition.

Recent scholars in religious studies have challenged the binary opposition between religion and secularity. For them, secularity names something that cannot be understood as simply the absence or diminution of religion. Secularity emerged from the complicated history of Christian ideas and practices, and has taken its place as a particular sort of "religious" phenomenon. Secularity has a cluster of constituent values, interests, assumptions, and biases that have greatly influenced (some would say, coerced) modern societies. Although secular advocates tend to portray their values as the simple products of reason, critics frame them as beliefs—beliefs that have driven the enormous political and economic influence of secularity. Secularity in this sense cannot be understood as the neutral, progressive, benevolent force championed by Dawkins, Harris, and others. It preaches toleration and rational advancement toward human prosperity; but it creates conditions in which intolerance thrives (as conspicuously evident in post-9/11 Islamophobia) and unequal distribution of resources becomes the norm.

For some theorists, although we have lived for a long time in a secular age, social conditions have changed enough that we should now refer to a "postsecular" age. Others retain "secular" as the preferred term. These debates over terminology are interesting, but in the end they may not matter so much. "Postsecular" shares the ambiguity that attaches to other famous "posts," notably "postmodern" and "postcolonial." When we call something postmodern, as Louis Menand frames the question, does that mean it has advanced beyond the modern and can be positioned *after* the modern—or has it been so indelibly influenced by the modern that it can never shed that influence?[25] Does the prefix "post," in other words, indicate a separation or an enduring connection? "Postsecular" is likely to retain a similar ambiguity, even if it becomes the dominant term. Perhaps the two most influential senior theorists of secularity are Talal Asad and Charles Taylor. Asad, an anthropologist and a convert to Islam, has written a number of essays in which he challenges the supposed religious and political neutrality of modern secular culture. The secular, he argues, is neither "continuous with the religious that supposedly preceded it . . . nor a simple break from it (that is, it is not the opposite, an essence that excludes the sacred). I take the secular to be a concept that brings together certain behaviors, knowledges, and sensibilities in modern life."[26] In the aftermath of 9/11, Asad saw the manifestations of secular culture all too clearly in "explosions of intolerance" that seemed "entirely compatible with secularism in a highly modern society."[27] Taylor, like Asad, takes a critical approach to modern secularity; and like Asad, he does so from the vantage point of someone with religious convictions who has seen those convictions put under secular stress. (Taylor is a faithful Catholic.) Taylor defines three versions of secularity. The first two have to do with the retreat and repression of religion, but he puts the greatest emphasis on what he calls "secular 3." "We have moved from a world in which the place of fullness was understood as unproblematically outside of or 'beyond' human life, to a conflicted age in which this construal is challenged by others which place it (in a wide range of different ways) 'within' human life."[28] In Taylor's secular 3, anyone's beliefs about immanence (meaning resides "within human life") or transcendence (meaning resides "beyond human life") are just one option among many granted cultural credibility. Beliefs once taken for granted have become "fragilized" in this secular age. As Michael Warner and his coeditors sort it out, Taylor believes that a great many people find themselves "cross-pressured, pulled in both directions, caught up somewhere between an 'open' and a 'closed' perspective on the world."[29]

Taylor's "cross-pressures" help to frame what I am calling entanglements of religion and secularity. Whatever their differences, recent scholars of secularity all dispute a clean separation of the religious from the secular. Tracy Fessenden, for example, has analyzed nineteenth-century American literary texts to see how religious values intrude on secular territory. She shows how currents of older religious thinking—specifically, Protestant beliefs and practices—helped to shape the supposedly "modern" thinking of nineteenth-century American writers like Harriet Beecher Stowe. Stowe, Fessenden argues, was tapping into anti-Catholic rhetoric as she made her case against slavery. The old religious elements significantly but quietly influenced the new antislavery advocacy.[30]

My approach in *Something Old, Something New* aligns with this recent scholarly inclination to deconstruct the binary opposition between religion and secularity. It would be a misstep, however, simply to displace the classic concept of secularity first articulated in the nineteenth century and still very much alive in contemporary discourse. "There exists a staggering multiplicity of secularisms," cautions Jacques Berlinerblau, and we ought to pay attention to all of them—whether "liberal or conservative," "brutish or benevolent," "friendly to religion, or hostile."[31]

OVERVIEW

Each of the chapters in this book examines a topic of contemporary relevance in which something old, affiliated with religious beliefs and practices, becomes entangled with something new and secular. Primary topics come from Christian institutions—especially

Catholicism, the oldest and largest of Christian churches, with the most eventful history—because these are the traditions I know best. Other religions do come into play, however, as they did briefly in the stem cell discussion above. Islam and Buddhism in particular enter as subtopics, in chapters 4 and 7 respectively.

"The Rhetoric of New Atheism" looks closely at the work of scientists and philosophers who think of themselves as new and defiantly secular, but who use old-fashioned rhetorical devices to supplement their scientific arguments. Although scientific arguments based on cause and effect reasoning explain a great deal, cause and effect reasoning by itself cannot answer the ultimate cosmological question: why does the world exist? As Richard Dawkins, Sam Harris, Daniel Dennett, and the like make their cases against God, with some of their tropes—notably pathopoeia, catachresis, and metalepsis—new atheists find themselves appropriating the pathos and prestige of the old religious discourse they hope to supplant. "The Rhetoric of Faithful Science" is a companion piece to "The Rhetoric of New Atheism." Here I explore the work of three prominent scientists, all devout Christians, who believe that scientific arguments are perfectly compatible with theism. Geneticist Francis Collins, Astronomer Owen Gingerich, and physicist-turned-priest John Polkinghorne make no attempt to separate the discourses of science and religion; instead, they use their scientific knowledge to mount a case for belief in God. The marriage of new science and old religion proves far from perfect, however, as the scientists' rhetoric reveals important defects in their apologetic projects. Their attempts to merge the newest developments in physics and genetics with old Christian beliefs produce moments of inconsistency and discontinuity.

In the next two chapters, other aspects of contemporary secularity come into focus. In both chapters, secularity means a new sort of cultural pluralism, and an elevated (some would say, "politically correct") degree of religious toleration. "Christians and Adversaries in the Evolving *Norton Anthology of English Literature*: Old-Time Religion and the New Academic Market" tracks changes in the famous anthology's annotations across nine editions. A pattern emerges in editors' notes about religious matters—in particular, about three versions of what were traditionally considered adversaries, from a Christian point of view: Satan, Islam, and Queer Sexuality. Early editions tend to reflect the views of Christian insiders, for an academic market still loosely associated with Christian monoculture. As cultural assumptions gradually moved in the direction of greater secularity and religious pluralism, the old annotations needed to be significantly revised to meet the conditions of the new market. The editors found themselves still bound to explicate the Christian truths embedded in works like *The Faerie Queene* and *Paradise Lost*, but their new secular perspectives entangled with the old literature to produce some complicated interpretive effects. "The Curious Case of Pope Francis" focuses on the pope's seemingly paradoxical attachment both to contemporary secular values and to conspicuously old-fashioned elements of Catholic devotion. This pope is at once very new and very old. Francis the New is more tolerant of diverse beliefs and lifestyles, more politically liberal, and more engaged with science than his predecessors; Francis the Old prays fervently over ancient, dubious relics and believes wholeheartedly in Satan as an agent in the world. How might we understand these strange entanglements of old and new in the popular, controversial pope? Do they indicate a divided or a unified purpose?

The last two chapters pair something old from Catholic tradition and something new from experiments in psychology and psychiatry. In "The Seven Deadly Sins: *Summa Theologica* Meets *Scientific American*," something old means the comprehensive volume of Church theology compiled by Thomas Aquinas in the thirteenth century, and something new a set of essays from *Scientific American* that describe contemporary experiments in cognitive science relevant to the seven deadly sins. The old *Summa* and the new *Scientific American* become entangled more compellingly than one might have expected. Aquinas's arguments, heavily influenced by Aristotle, anticipate complications that will persist in modern scientific approaches to virtue and vice. The cognitive scientists often reinscribe the old theological values even as they secularize symptoms and consequences. "Psychedelic Last Rites," fittingly placed at the end, compares the Catholic sacrament of extreme unction with modern experiments in which dying subjects receive psychedelic drugs as therapy for anxiety and depression. The old and the new "sacraments" share a fundamental purpose: to fortify the spirits and alleviate the psychological distress of people as they near the end of their lives. Given this grave responsibility, the psychiatrists in charge of the psychedelic trials often compromise scientific rigor in deference to the quasi-sacramental status of their experiments. This last chapter, perhaps more distinctly than any other, shows how something new and secular joins the high purpose of something old and religious, even as it attempts to replace it.

Chapter 2

The Rhetoric of New Atheism

New atheists face an old problem as they mount their cases against the existence of God: scientific truth, founded on cause-effect reasoning, cannot deliver a clinching causal argument. The ultimate cosmological question cannot be answered. Why is there anything here at all? Like their religious antagonists, new atheists find themselves positing that *something* must simply exist as the foundation of our universe. The question of "what caused this" necessarily slips into infinite regress; either God or some rudimentary version of the natural world must be granted exemption from the cause-effect requirement. Scientific reasoning cannot take us all the way down.

I would characterize this problem as the "aporia" of new atheism. Aporia, which means roughly "impasse" at its root, is a Greek rhetorical trope that poststructuralists renovated for their weightier hermeneutical purposes. In its simpler rhetorical sense, aporia describes a moment when doubt stalls a speaker as he or she puzzles over how to proceed with an argument. (For the Greeks and their Renaissance disciples, this expression of doubt may be either genuine or feigned.) Poststructuralists appropriated the term to name that site where a text undermines its authority in the very act of trying to establish it. The poststructuralist aporia is serious business, not merely a tool in the rhetorical workshop. Although new atheists have no patience with poststructuralist critiques of scientific epistemology, the aporia they face has the feel of deconstructive paradox. Scientific reasoning cannot quite seal the deal: what else might serve? The new atheists tacitly compensate for this aporia by deploying rhetorical devices to supplement science proper.

"New atheism" has not been defined very precisely, and some of the writers I include under this rubric would not see themselves as part of a coherent school. Both Jim Holt and Alan Lightman, for instance, criticize other new atheists, but for matters of attitude and tone rather than substantive conviction. Both of them unambiguously assert their atheism. As I will use the term, new atheists share three features. First, they all write in the aftermath of September 11, 2001. Either explicitly or implicitly, they react against the religious ideas that helped motivate those attacks. Arguably the first of the new atheists, Sam Harris says he "began writing this book [*The End of Faith*] on September 12, 2001."[1] Second, new atheists all reject the compromise position called "NOMA," short for "Non-Overlapping Magisteria," which preempts entanglement by treating science and religion as separate domains of inquiry. Stephen Jay Gould identified himself as an atheist, but for him and other NOMA advocates, science and religion ask and answer different sets of questions.[2] The two domains of inquiry can coexist peacefully. New atheists do not accept the NOMA compromise: for them, scientific reasoning overlaps significantly with religious thinking. What science discovers clearly impacts religious beliefs. A third feature of new atheism is its public boldness about a subject once considered taboo, or in any event a matter of private conviction. Earlier atheists tended to show more reserve and deference than is evident in the new generation. If new atheists differ in the tone they use to address the religious mainstream—some, like Lightman, maintain a gentle détente, while many others, including

Richard Dawkins, passionately attack believers—they all write with a new sense of cultural confidence. And certainly their books have found a broad popular audience.

For all their confidence, the new atheists cannot simply ignore the cosmological aporia that lurks at the base of their arguments and quietly entangles them with theists. In this chapter I will focus first on their efforts to address this aporia, then analyze their use of several tropes to make atheist arguments more attractive: paralepsis; the sarcasm cluster (apodioxis, tapinosis, diasyrmus); pathopoeia; and the linked tropes of catachresis and metalepsis. Each of these rhetorical devices, labeled with its old-school Greek name, deviates from strictly scientific reasoning even as it serves the ends of rational science. Especially with pathopoeia, catachresis, and metalepsis, new atheists find themselves entangled with the religious discourse they mean to supplant.

APORIA

All of the new atheists concede at some point that they cannot answer the most basic cosmological question: why does the world exist? (Or alternatively, why is there something rather than nothing?) Harris briefly engages the question and files it away as "a mystery absolute," forever opaque to rational inquiry.[3] Holt is the only new atheist to embrace the mystery with open arms. In *Why Does the World Exist? An Existential Detective Story*, he interviews scientists, philosophers, and theologians; he ends up elucidating the aporia but does not uncover a detective who can solve the mystery. One promising candidate is Oxford physicist David Deutsch. He first brushes aside Holt's question with a joke. Why is there something rather than nothing? "Even if there was nothing, you'd still be complaining!"[4] But then Deutsch gives a more serious description of the aporia as a "brick wall":

"I don't think that an ultimate explanation of reality is possible," he said, shaking his head. "That doesn't mean I think there's a *limit* to what we can explain. We'll never run into a brick wall which says, 'NO EXPLANATION BEYOND THIS POINT.' On the other hand, I don't think we'll find a brick wall that says, 'THIS IS THE ULTIMATE EXPLANATION FOR EVERYTHING.' In fact, those two brick walls would be almost the same. If, *qua impossibile*, you were to have an ultimate explanation, it would mean the philosophical problem of why *that* was the true explanation—why reality was this way and not another—would be forever insoluble."[5]

Deutsch uses the aporia-friendly metaphor of an impassable brick wall, but he does so with some discomfort. There is no brick wall, he begins, but as he thinks about it, there might as well be—if "beyond the wall" means finding the answer to why we have the world we have. Holt hears something similar from physicist Steven Weinberg. Like Deutsch, Weinberg has great expertise in an area of science that might one day describe the original conditions of the universe (quantum mechanics and the multiverse); but like Deutsch, Weinberg concedes that the final causal question cannot be answered. When Holt asks "why this huge assemblage of universes should exist," Weinberg simply replies, "I don't see any way out of *that* mystery."[6] Elsewhere Weinberg shows that he does take the (unanswerable) mystery seriously, even as he dismisses religious belief as more harmful than beneficial. He understands human curiosity about ultimate purpose, but he rejects any defense of a benevolent deity who would permit something as atrocious as the Holocaust: "It seems a bit unfair to my relatives to be murdered in order to provide an opportunity for free will for Germans, but even putting that aside, how does free will account for cancer?"[7]

Another prominent physicist and new atheist, Lawrence Krauss has no patience at all with suggestions of cosmological impasse. In fact, Krauss's title—*A Universe from Nothing: Why There Is Something Rather Than Nothing*—seems to promise a definitive answer. But it turns out that he cannot make good on that promise. He presents a fascinating set of theories that indicate our traditional notion of "nothing" actually amounts to "something" in the world of quantum physics. He grudgingly concedes, however, "this does beg the possible question, of what, if anything, fixed the rules that governed such creation."[8] Krauss does not find the question interesting and barely includes it (near the end of his book). In his preface to the paperback edition, he confesses his exasperation over reviewers who have used the ultimate question against him, and offers a testy sort of concession:

> Can one ever say anything other than the fact that the nothing that became our something was a part of "something" else, in which the potential for our existence, or any existence, was always implicit? In this book I take a rather flippant attitude toward this concern, because I don't think it adds anything to the productive discussion. . . . No doubt some will view this as my own limitations, and maybe it is.[9]

Krauss finds the brick wall, in other words, and shows no interest in what might lie behind it. If that is not good enough for you, he sneers, "Write your own book."[10] The aporia annoys Krauss, amuses Deutsch, and makes Weinberg somber.

New atheists sometimes touch on two other fundamental questions that science has not solved: How did life begin? What is the nature of consciousness? But they distinguish these two problems from the ultimate cosmological question. The origins of life and consciousness, they believe, will eventually be solved by scientific investigation. Dawkins acknowledges that natural selection becomes relevant only after life begins, which rules out a Darwinian explanation of the origin of life. We may have needed a "stroke of luck" for life to start up, he says, an event that was "statistically improbable," but it only had to happen once—and natural selection took it from there. Similarly, "[t]he origin of consciousness might be another major gap whose bridging was of the same order of improbability" as life.[11] Our world includes life and consciousness, however improbable their origins, and the new atheists have confidence that chemistry and neuroscience will sort out the causes. Life and consciousness present gaps to be bridged, not an aporetic wall.

PARALEPSIS

Of all the rhetorical devices used by new atheists to supplement scientific reason, paralepsis is the simplest and most rarely deployed. But it works quite well. The term comes from Greek roots meaning to leave something aside. When speakers use paralepsis, they state that someone or something is not worth talking about: a subject is raised but only to dismiss it. Paralepsis amounts to a version of irony, because in pretending to pass over a subject, a speaker actually draws particular attention to it. As Henry Peacham describes it in *The Garden of Eloquence*, "Paralepsis, of some called Praeteritio, of others Occupatio, and it is when the Orator faineth and maketh as though he would say nothing in some matter, when notwithstanding he speaketh most of all, or when he saith some thing: in saying he will not say it."[12]

The new atheist who deploys paralepsis most strikingly is Alain de Botton. In *Religion for Atheists*, he dismisses as tedious all argument for or against the existence of God. He cannot be bothered to wade into the subject. "The most boring and unproductive question one can ask of any religion is whether or not it is *true*," he begins the book. "To save time, and at the risk of losing readers painfully early on in this project, let us bluntly state that of course no religions are true in any God-given sense."[13] De Botton's paralepsis achieves his purpose in three ways. First, he leverages the handy phrase "of course" to confirm that the question of God's existence has long been settled by the (boring) arguments of those who have come before. It needs no discussion now because it is perfectly obvious. Paralepsis offers an unassailable verdict because it rules out consideration of evidence. Second, de Botton invites all readers to join his elite club—"let *us* bluntly state . . ."—or else concede their unworthiness by caring about a pointless, archaic argument. And third, he leavens all this with humorous self-deprecation that actually reinforces his elitism: I am so brash in my truth telling that most people will not be able to handle it.

Other new atheists, for the most part, want to earn their victories by going into all the details de Botton sweeps aside. But paralepsis still proves useful now and then. Philosopher Daniel Dennett dismisses as fruitless the process of arguing with believers:

> Many of us brights [atheists] have devoted considerable time and energy at some point in our lives to looking at the arguments for and against the existence of God, and many brights continue to pursue these issues, hacking away vigorously at the arguments of the believers as if they were trying to refute a rival scientific

theory. But not I. I decided some time ago that diminishing returns had set in on the arguments about God's existence, and I doubt that any breakthroughs are in the offing, from either side.[14]

He declines the debate, but with a weary condescension. Believers obviously have nothing like a "scientific theory" to compete with the reasonable brights. Refuting them would be easy enough but accomplish nothing. Once again, through paralepsis, a new atheist pretends to pass over debate about God, but achieves a preemptive rhetorical effect of making atheism seem the obvious right answer. Bill Maher does something similar near the beginning of his documentary *Religulous*. He breezily dismisses any arguments about the big questions of why we are here: "My big thing is 'I don't know,'" he tells viewers. "That's what I preach."[15] Technically, Maher would count as agnostic, but his antireligious zeal aligns him securely with the new atheists. Like them, he invites us to bypass detailed argument and join the brights without delay. He spends much of the film interviewing loopy advocates of faith-based silliness.

THE SARCASM CLUSTER: APODIOXIS, TAPINOSIS, DIASYRMUS

Maher's *Religulous* exploits a number of easy targets for ridicule— but he is a comedian, after all, not a scientist or philosopher, and the film makes no claim to offer a balanced slate of religious representatives. Many of the scientists and philosophers who write as new atheists share Maher's appetite for sarcasm. Richard Sherry in *A Treatise of Schemes and Tropes* defines sarcasm as "jesting or scoffing bitingly."[16] New atheists frequently frame an opponent's argument as ridiculous or absurd on the face of it. Greek rhetoric has many terms and categories for this sort of strategy; the three listed above seem most useful for analyzing how the new atheists gain an edge through some form of mockery.

Apodioxis offers the broadest stroke in this cluster of tropes: a speaker rejects the opponent's argument as obviously absurd. In Peacham's phrasing, apodioxis means "to reject vaine and fond arguments of an adversary: namely such as are unworthy of answere."[17] Christopher Hitchens is the laureate of apodioxis among the new atheists. Often he rejects faith-based arguments with a sweeping, contemptuous dismissal:

> One must state it plainly. Religion comes from the period of human prehistory where nobody—not even the mighty Democritus who concluded that all matter was made from atoms—had the smallest idea what was going on. It comes from the bawling and fearful infancy of our species, and is a babyish attempt to meet our inescapable demand for knowledge (as well as for comfort, reassurance, and other infantile needs). Today the least educated of my children knows much more about the natural order than any of the founders of religion, and one would like to think—though the connection is not a fully demonstrable one—that this is why they seem so uninterested in sending fellow humans to hell.[18]

Hitchens means to entertain atheists as well as infuriate believers, and he surely recognizes that hyperbolic passages such as this one will do both. Religious arguments are too "babyish" to deserve serious consideration. The mention of Democritus, which might seem to undermine his point, actually adds a layer of atheist self-congratulation. Democritus earns the epithet "mighty" because his atomism provided a foundation for the proto-atheism of Epicurus and Lucretius. Hitchens caps this section with an apodioxic flourish: "All attempts to reconcile faith with science and reason are consigned to failure and ridicule."[19] Not even scientific prominence can safeguard a believer. Hitchens rejects the ideas of "ex-agnostic" astronomer Fred Hoyle as "the same old mumbo-jumbo."[20] With similar rhetoric, Krauss brushes aside a complex theological argument as "semantic hocus-pocus."[21]

A more specific trope of sarcasm known as tapinosis amounts to a kind of name-calling. From a root meaning "demeaning" or "humbling," tapinosis substitutes a debased, conspicuously diminished word or phrase for the proper term. Like apodioxis, tapinosis serves as much to entertain atheists as provoke the religious. Harris offers a nice example: "Jesus Christ—who, as it turns out, was born of a virgin, cheated death, and rose bodily into the heavens—can now be eaten in the form of a cracker."[22] He cleverly demeans the sacramental vehicle by substituting "cracker" for "host." If he had used a plainer word like "bread" to name the object in question, the sarcasm would lose its edge. The word "bread" takes on allegorical meanings readily (e.g., "I am the bread of life"). A cracker has no comparable gravitas: the word looks and sounds funny, and it carries pejorative connotations, at least outside the world of snacks. Hitchens deploys tapinosis when he refers to St. Francis as a "mammal": "[Ockham] was a Franciscan (in other words, an acolyte of the aforementioned mammal who was said to have preached to birds)."[23] Hitchens likes to cast the religious as "babyish" and primitive; reducing St. Francis to his animal class removes his dignity and encourages bright readers to laugh at anything associated with him. De Botton uses a gentler tapinosis at the start of his book. In the caption to his first full-page picture—a painting of St. Agnes of Montepulciano, who was credited with levitation and bringing dead children back to life—De Botton writes, "Probably just a very nice person."[24] Dawkins's name-calling tropes differ sharply from De Botton's, and even from Harris's "cracker" and Hitchens's "mammal," which are relatively subtle by comparison. There is nothing subtle about Dawkins's renamings of God. God becomes, to cite a few examples, a "sky-fairy," a "bloke," a "Divine Knob-Twiddler," "the monster of the Bible," and a "psychotic delinquent."[25] This last one, to be fair, purports to describe only the God of the Old Testament.

One last trope of the sarcastic sort, diasyrmus, mocks a subject by means of a ridiculous comparison. Many new atheists delight in the creative opportunities offered by diasyrmus. Because careful argument is not the point here, they have a free hand to invent laughable analogies with religious beliefs. More than any other trope, diasyrmus shows new atheists acting as comedians; the best examples are quite entertaining. Harris reflects that although believers have been conditioned to accept the most absurd assertions of their faith, they would be as skeptical as anyone of similar absurdities put forward as truth—such as the proposition, say, "that frozen yogurt can make a man invisible."[26] Like his "cracker" tapinosis, this remark shows nice comic flair: frozen yogurt is just funnier in this context than regular yogurt, probably because it has less cultural dignity. Dawkins ridicules theologians by comparing their profession to those of lesser intellectual status. He recalls a moment when an Oxford astronomer answered a deep cosmological question, "Ah, now we move beyond the realm of science. This is where I have to hand over to our good friend the chaplain." Dawkins continues, "I was not quick-witted enough to utter the response I later wrote: 'But why the chaplain? Why not the gardener or the chef?' "[27] Dennett once likens religious belief to tobacco smoking. Religion may eventually be heavily discouraged as a practice, he speculates, but still tolerated, "since there are those who say they can't live without it."[28] Both Harris and Dawkins use comic cross-paradigm comparisons to mock Biblical literalists about the age of the universe. "This means that 120 million of us place the big bang 2,500 years *after* the Babylonians and Sumerians learned to brew beer."[29] A fundamentalist teacher holds the view that "the entire universe began after the domestication of the dog."[30] Together these evoke the absurd (but cute) image of a divine creator sitting somewhere sipping a beer and patting his Golden Retriever.

Sometimes the new atheists use diasyrmus for gentler satirical effects. Dennett, for example, compares organized religions to sports teams: "In this scenario, being a member of a religion becomes more and more like being a Boston Red Sox fan, or a Dallas Cowboys fan. Different colors, different songs and cheers, different symbols, and vigorous competition—would you want your daughter to marry a Yankee fan?"[31] Harris refers to religious disputes between Indians and Pakistanis over " 'facts' that are every bit as fanciful as the names of Santa's reindeer."[32] Several other new atheists also bring up Santa as a fantasy comparable to belief in God. The Santa and sports comparisons have a mocking effect, to be sure, but they also show the potential downside of such rhetorical gestures. A potential atheist who laughs wholeheartedly at frozen yogurt superpowers may well reflect that our collective Santa fantasy is pleasant, productive, and endearing. The diasyrmus meant to ridicule might backfire: who wants to get rid of Santa, or the Red Sox? Or even the Dallas Cowboys?

PATHOPOEIA

As entertaining as they are, the tropes of sarcasm can only accomplish so much for the new atheists. With these tactics, as with paralepsis, it may seem that no real entanglement is taking place. The smug tropes of paralepsis and sarcasm circumvent and parody religious ideas instead of seriously engaging with them. If entanglement can be detected here, it is only in the shadowy sense of repressed content. Paralepsis and sarcasm repress but do not eradicate the religious other as an entangled partner. The serious claims of faith loom as a sort of textual unconscious, a force that might challenge atheist complacency if brought out into the open. The aporia, after all, persists at the bottom of secular arguments and mitigates their rational advantages over theism. With the tropes of pathopoeia, catachresis, and metalepsis, new atheist rhetoric betrays a more robust entanglement with religious discourse and a greater appetite for something to supplement scientific reasoning.

Pathopoeia adds a dimension to new atheist rhetoric that is more serious, moving, and (usually) quite personal. A speaker uses pathopoeia to arouse strong emotions in the audience. According to John Smith in *The Mystery of Rhetoric Unveil'd*, "Pathopoeia is a form of speech whereby the speaker moves the mind of his hearers to some vehemency of affection, as of love, hatred, gladness, sorrow, &c. It is when the speaker himself (being inwardly moved with any of those deep and vehement affections) doth by evident demonstration, passionate pronunciation and suitable gestures make a lively expression thereof."[33]

The most effective instances of pathopoeia in new atheism emerge from personal narratives that stir deep emotions, especially sorrow and fear. One exception comes at the beginning of Harris's book, where he aims to arouse fear, but does so with a narrative that does not come from his direct experience. A religious terrorist is about to blow himself up in a crowded bus: "The young man boards the bus as it leaves the terminal. . . . His pockets are filled with nails, ball bearings, and rat poison. . . . The couple at his side appears to be shopping for a new refrigerator. The woman has decided on a model, but her husband worries that it will be too expensive."[34] Harris adds relatable details of the couple to make us care more about their imminent deaths. The End of Faith more generally prompts us to fear the apocalyptic consequences of believers equipped with nuclear weapons. It is not just isolated unlucky couples we need to worry about. "The days of our religious identities are clearly numbered," he says at the end of the book. "Whether the days of civilization itself are numbered would seem to depend, rather too much, on how soon we realize this."[35] Maher's film ends on a similar note of warning. As he stands at the supposed site of Armageddon, he explains that such a mythical apocalyptic event could actually happen—a self-fulfilling prophecy—unless we free ourselves from religious absurdities.

The most moving instances of new atheist pathopoeia, however, are subtler and more personal. One minor example of personal pathopoeia comes in an uncharacteristically sentimental passage from Dawkins. As he remembers his first "convert" to atheism, the late Douglas Adams (author of The Hitchhiker's Guide to the Galaxy), Dawkins invites our sympathy with this elegiac apostrophe: "Douglas, I miss you. You are my cleverest, funniest, most open-minded, wittiest, tallest, and possibly only convert. I hope this book might have made you laugh—though not as much as you made me."[36] He poignantly uses the present tense to address his friend. The sarcastic, combative Dawkins shows an emotional softness here that gives atheism more of a heart. You do not have to believe in God, the passage implies, to feel the kind of love promised by religious communities.

De Botton includes a moment of autobiographical pathopoeia that hints at deeper emotions. In his introductory chapter, he writes about his father, "I was brought up in a committedly atheistic household, as the son of two secular Jews who placed religious belief somewhere on a par with an attachment to Santa Claus. I recall my father reducing my sister to tears in an attempt to dislodge her modestly held notion that a reclusive god might dwell somewhere in the universe. She was eight years old at the time."[37] His sister's tears suggest a problematic relationship with the elder de Botton, who comes off badly for rejecting his little girl's imagination of some other sort of father—a cosmic anchor she apparently finds comfort in. De Botton lets his sister provide the emotion in this little anecdote, but in the next paragraph, he returns to the subject of his father. "In my mid-twenties I underwent a crisis of faithlessness," he writes. He loved religious art and longed to engage with it, despite his unshakable commitment to atheism. A subtly pathopoetic moment comes when he talks about his father's death: "It was not until my father had been dead for several years—and buried under a Hebrew headstone in a Jewish cemetery in Willesden, north-west London, because he had, intriguingly, omitted to make more secular arrangements— that I began to face up to the full scale of my ambivalence regarding the doctrinaire principles with which I had been inculcated in childhood."[38] Here the sadness associated with the loss of his father joins with inchoate transatheistic emotions. Neither he nor his father moves away from atheism, but both find themselves "intriguingly" engaged with symbols of the religious life they cannot embrace.

Two other moments of pathopoeia—one in Holt, one in Lightman—present the most complex expressions of personal emotion in the new atheist oeuvre. In both cases, a personal narrative supplements and almost displaces scientific reason. Holt's and Lightman's books have a literary richness that distinguishes them from the others. This should come as no surprise: Lightman works at MIT not only as a physicist, but as a practicing novelist and teacher of writing; and Holt, although well-versed in math, logic, and physics, writes literary nonfiction.

The most intensely pathopoetic moment in new atheism comes as Holt narrates a personal story that interrupts his project. He has traveled to Austin to interview physicist Steven Weinberg, one of his most authoritative and promising subjects. Weinberg has excellent scientific credentials as well as the broader philosophical perspective necessary to address Holt's question: why does the world exist? The night before he is to meet Weinberg, Holt learns that his beloved dog "Renzo" is suffering seizures from metastasized cancer. He postpones the interview and flies home to comfort Renzo in his last few days.

Before he heard the news about Renzo, Holt had spent a pensive afternoon and evening in Texas. He walks around the noisy, "beery" streets of Austin and begins to feel existential angst:

Making my way through the cacophonous crush under the hot sun, I pretended that I was Roquentin, the existential hero of Sartre's novel *Nausea*. I tried to summon up the disgust he would feel at the surfeit of Being that overflowed the streets of Austin— at its sticky thickness, its grossness, its absurd contingency. Whence did it all spring? How did the ignoble mess around me triumph over pristine Nothingness?[39]

Holt expresses a gnostic revulsion from the carnival of bodily life, perhaps triggered by a simpler feeling of loneliness. His sense of alienation sharpens because "everyone around me seemed to be having an awfully good time."[40] Even the famous Austin bats refuse to perform for him. In an effort to elevate and dignify his malaise, he salutes "pristine Nothingness"; the phrase suggests Buddhist emptiness and detachment as well as the existentialism he has been imitating.

His pose of detachment lasts only until he gets the news about his dog. Now "nothingness" becomes something terrible: "Renzo's once-rich canine sensory world had disappeared into nothingness. All he could do was blindly stumble around in circles, whimpering in distress. Only when I held him in my arms did he seem to get some relief."[41] He sits with Renzo as the veterinarian euthanizes him. Holt makes no attempt to moderate the pathos or retreat into a cooler, *New Yorker*-style sophistication. Instead he maximizes the emotional effects. When the vet injects the lethal chemical, Renzo "exhaled in a burst. 'That was his last breath,' the vet said. Then he exhaled again, and was still. Good dog." Holt surrenders his dog's body for cremation, and then, "carrying only Renzo's blanket, I walked home. The next day, I called Steven Weinberg at his home in Austin to talk about why the world exists."[42] His pathopoetic interlude has given the ultimate question new weight and more urgency. It is as if Holt now *really needs* Weinberg to explain the point of this upsetting world. The pathos of Renzo's blanket calls for more than an aporetic shrug.

Lightman's most striking pathopoeia also develops from an animal story, this one about a nest of ospreys near his summer home in Maine. He and his wife had spent a lot of time studying the ospreys in the way scientists do: observing, measuring, counting, predicting. "After several years of cataloguing such data," he summarizes, "we felt that we knew these ospreys. . . . Reading our 'osprey journals' on a winter's night, we felt a sense of pride and satisfaction. We had carefully studied and documented a small part of the universe."[43] Then something happens that transforms Lightman's "pride and satisfaction" into sublime feelings of terror and awe. From the deck of his house, he watches two fledgling ospreys take their first flight:

They did a loop of my house and then headed straight at me with tremendous speed. My immediate impulse was to run for cover, since they could have ripped me apart with their powerful talons. But something held me to my ground. When they were within twenty feet of me, they suddenly veered upward and away. But before that dazzling and frightening vertical climb, for about half a second we made eye contact. Words cannot convey what was exchanged between us in that instant. It was a look of connectedness, of mutual respect, of recognition that we shared the same land. After they were gone, I found that I was shaking, and in tears. To this day, I do not understand what happened in that half second. But it was one of the most profound moments of my life.[44]

The event he narrates might seem trivial alongside Harris's bus explosion, but it is much more intense in its pathopoetic effects. A man who has mastered the universe through scientific knowledge abruptly finds himself vulnerable and speechless. Words fail him— even now, in retrospect—and he cannot "understand what happened." If this were simply a matter of physical threat, the emotion would be easy enough to understand. There must be more to it. The osprey moment includes not only a fear of bodily harm, but something of a more cosmic complexity. Lightman's emotion may come in part from a reversal of subject-object orientation: the ospreys, formerly objects of his study, suddenly become subjects looking at *him*, with indecipherable intentions. Any moment that transforms a person's sense of cosmic identity can arouse terror and inspiration all at once: panic and profundity. Such moments happen all the time to religious believers and users of psychedelic drugs, but it is unusual to see someone like Alan Lightman "shaking, and in tears" over an event that seems perfectly natural. He by no means compromises his atheist convictions in the aftermath of the osprey epiphany; in the same chapter, he reaffirms, "I am an atheist myself. I completely endorse the central doctrine of science."[45] But his sublime moment with the ospreys suggests that science by itself cannot account for the complexity of human experience. Our emotional reach, in other words, should exceed our scientific grasp. The better a new atheist can accommodate his convictions to our profoundest emotions, the more effective his appeal to those who have been conditioned to find those emotions only within religious discourse.

CATACHRESIS AND METALEPSIS

If Lightman found a way to fuse religion and science by means of pathopoeia, other new atheists achieve this effect through the linked (and complex) tropes of catachresis and metalepsis. It might be helpful to start with an example from Harris.

In his first chapter, "Reason in Exile," Harris urges humanity to recognize "the absurdities of most of our religious beliefs. I fear, however, that the time has not yet arrived. In this sense, what follows is written very much in the spirit of a prayer. I pray that" humans will awake to reason.[46] His use of "prayer" provides a clear example of catachresis. Like most words with the prefix "cata-," catachresis suggests trouble. It means that a speaker "misuses" a word by applying it outside of its proper realm of signification. Smith calls it an "abuse" (the Latin equivalent is *abusio*): "when words are too far wrested from their native and genuine signification." "For lack of a proper word," he continues, a speaker "borroweth the next or the likest to the thing that he would signify. . . . [It] is the expressing of one matter by the name of another, which is incompatible with, and sometimes clean contrary to it."[47] Some rhetoricians are kinder to catachresis, which they consider defensible if language does not contain a "proper" term for the speaker's intended meaning. A simple example from English would be our reference to "the legs of a table."

When Harris uses "prayer" and "I pray," he obviously "wrests" a word from its native discursive realm. He applies it in a context which is "incompatible with"—indeed, "clean contrary to"—its religious signification. In the act of denouncing religious faith, he summons a word that has radically religious meanings. Harris's catachresis would be defensible (rather than an "abuse") only if the new atheist had no scientific, secular word available for what he meant to say. I would argue that this is precisely the case. Harris borrows from religion the only word with sufficient gravitas and charm to signify the urgency of his appeal. By invoking prayer, he borrows the prestige of the supernatural in an attempt to eradicate all belief in the supernatural.

Harris's use of prayer could also be described as metalepsis. Metalepsis is harder to pin down than most tropes, but like catachresis, it means using words at some remove from their expected contexts. Metalepsis requires a hearer or reader to make interpretive connections that involve more than one figurative leap. When Harris says "I pray" that humans will renounce faith, we first register the proper sense of "pray," which means a communication between a person and God. But then we must move beyond this first trope (my words are a prayer) to a further trope: prayers are often caused by some sort of crisis, and such a crisis now compels me to write. Harold Bloom made metalepsis the sixth and climactic trope in his *Map of Misreading*. Bloom's use of metalepsis, somewhat idiosyncratic but well enough founded in classical rhetoric, provides a good key to the importance of this trope for new atheists. For Bloom, the final trope of misreading is "a metalepsis or transumption of the process of reading (and writing) poems, a final ratio of revision that I have named *apophrades*, or the return of the precursors."[48] In metalepsis, he argues, a later poet gains leverage over the great precursor by "substituting early words for late words"; and by this means, "the dead return, to be triumphed over by the living."[49] Harris uses the early word "prayer" to name something late. The great precursor, religious faith, reappears with its native vigor, but only to be "triumphed over" by new atheism.

Similar examples of catachresis and metalepsis can be found in many new atheist books. Another religious word Harris appropriates is "sacred": "Nothing is more sacred than the facts. No one should win any points in our discourse for deluding himself."[50] By giving "facts" the blessing of "sacred," he circumvents philosophical objections that might be raised about what constitutes a fact. Antifoundationalists would find his rhetoric clever but evasive. Dennett, too, borrows "sacred" to defend atheism against charges of disenchantment. "Is something sacred?" he asks. "Yes, I say with Nietzsche. I could not pray to it, but I can stand in affirmation of its magnificence. The world is sacred."[51] Dennett amplifies the effect by mentioning "the glory of nature."[52] Although Hitchens, like other new atheists, shies away from the word "miracle," he substitutes for it a word only slightly more secular, "wonder": "We have only recently established that a cow is closer in family to a whale than to a horse: other wonders certainly await us."[53] Even the pragmatic physicist Krauss finds "wonder" useful. "The universe is far stranger and far richer—more wondrously strange—than our meager human imaginations can anticipate."[54]

Lightman quotes and seems to endorse a remark by his friend that "science is the religion of the twenty-first century."[55] Harris asserts that "spirituality can be—indeed, must be—deeply rational."[56] In both statements, Bloom's metaleptic apophrades comes into full view. Religious faith returns, but only to the extent that it recognizes the triumph of rational science. Science, according to Harris, may one day help us answer the old religious question, "Is there life after death?"[57] Krauss offers physical explanations of the end of the world to replace the religious ideas of apocalypse. In one theory, "protons and neutrons will decay" and "matter will disappear"; in another, our unstable world will "recollapse inward to a point" and "our universe will then disappear as abruptly as it probably began."[58]

But the beginning of the universe remains a problem. All of these rhetorical maneuvers still leave intact the aporia with which we began: why does the world exist? This was the title of Holt's book, and it is Holt who offers one final, thought-provoking instance of metalepsis. It comes as he is reviewing the efforts of physicists to discover a "final theory," which "promises to go far beyond our current physics in clarifying the origins of the universe."[59] But even scientists like Stephen Hawking and Alex Vilenkin, optimists about the prospects for a final theory, do not hold out hope for progress with Holt's ultimate question:

[A final theory] might, for instance, show how space and time emerged from still more fundamental entities that we as yet have no conception of. But it is hard to see how even a final theory could explain why there is a universe instead of nothing at all. Are the laws of physics somehow to inform the Abyss that it is pregnant with Being? If so, where do the laws themselves live? Do they hover over the world like the mind of God, commanding it to exist?[60]

Holt's metalepsis revives his great precursor in theodicy, John Milton—unmistakably, although without any direct mention of him. He echoes these early lines from *Paradise Lost*, where Milton addresses the Holy Spirit:

> Thou from the first
> Wast present, and with mighty wings outspread
> Dove-like sat'st brooding on the vast abyss
> And mad'st it pregnant ... (1.19–22).[61]

Milton himself is echoing the account of creation at the start of the Bible. Milton's God becomes, in Holt's trope, "the laws of physics." Both of them make "the Abyss ... pregnant with Being." Holt knows that the comparison cannot really work, at least for minds that have shed faith. It offers no relief from the stubborn aporia of beginnings. But by assimilating Milton, he does earn a rhetorical advantage: he borrows the prestige and inspiration of a man who, like the new atheists, set out to rewrite Genesis.

Chapter 3

The Rhetoric of Faithful Science

The subtitle of Francis Collins's bestselling counterattack on new atheism encodes a bold premise: *The Language of God: A Scientist Presents Evidence for Belief.* Milder sallies against Richard Dawkins and company, like Amir Aczel's *Why Science Does Not Disprove God,* argue merely that the logic of science cannot mount a decisive case against theism. When Stephen Jay Gould separated scientific and religious thinking as Non-Overlapping Magisteria (NOMA), he thereby removed scientific evidence from relevance to theological argument. Collins, along with the other authors I would call faithful scientists, makes a stronger claim. They will use the knowledge they have gathered as working scientists to prove—or more humbly, to present compelling evidence—that God exists. Faithful scientists refuse to cede the territory of science to new atheists. Entanglement is built into their project: for them, scientific materialism ultimately partners with the religious faith it may seem to displace.

From over a dozen respectable books that fit under the label of faithful science, I have chosen to focus on three that seem particularly sophisticated and well argued. Perhaps the best known, most influential of these is Collins's *The Language of God.* Collins, an accomplished geneticist, came to prominence as head of the Human Genome Project. He was an atheist as a graduate student, but reading and reflection led him to change his mind and convert to Christianity. Owen Gingerich had a highly successful career at Harvard as a professor of astronomy and the history of science. A devout Mennonite, he was invited in 2005 to deliver the Noble Lectures at Harvard, which became the short book *God's Universe*. The third book is John Polkinghorne's *Science and Religion in Quest of Truth*. Polkinghorne was a distinguished professor of particle physics at Cambridge for twenty-five years, before studying theology and becoming ordained as an Anglican priest.

The three books differ in tone and emphasis. Polkinghorne focuses dispassionately on scientific and theological arguments, whereas Collins weaves in ample personal narrative along with frank emotional content. Gingerich includes only a few personal moments, but he likes to mix in poetic subtexts. Gingerich is somewhat more tentative in the style of his argument than either Polkinghorne or Collins. But all three books reject NOMA as well as the notion that science is inherently inimical to religious belief. All three faithful scientists use scientific ideas to persuade readers that belief in God is a more rational conviction than atheism.

Gingerich recalls a television series he was asked to develop in response to Carl Sagan's popular *Cosmos*. Sagan's show "offered a conspicuously materialist approach to the universe," Gingerich writes, whereas his show would integrate scientific ideas with theistic approaches.[1] *Space, Time, and God* never made it to production, but planning six episodes helped Gingerich "focus my thoughts on the basic issues where science and religion intersect. . . . Rather than dwell on historical conflicts between science and religion, the program would have pointed out that the Judeo-Christian framework has proved to be a particularly fertile ground for the rise of modern science."[2] Polkinghorne agrees, adding that theology "should be gratefully attentive to all that science can tell it about the universe's nature and history."[3] Those who are able to combine scientific and religious knowledge will benefit from a "binocular vision onto reality" and discover truth "that is deeper and more comprehensive than either discipline could offer on its own. This is the premise on which the enquiry pursued in this book is based, presented as an expression of its author's belief in the ultimate unity of knowledge."[4] Collins declares a similar purpose. Given the "stridency" and unworthiness of contemporary debate on science and religion, "many choose to reject both the trustworthiness of scientific conclusion and the value of organized religion, slipping instead into various forms of antiscientific thinking, shallow spirituality, or simple apathy."[5] He wants to transform the debate by showing how his fully informed scientific mind harmonizes with his deep faith as a Christian.

The faithful scientists concede that Christianity has not always done a good job of appreciating the work of scientists. They cite the case of Galileo as a conspicuous lapse. But they also note that recent popes have done much to repair the relationship between theology and science. Pius XII was an early and enthusiastic supporter of the Big Bang theory, and he endorsed most elements of evolutionary theory (amended to include the mysterious infusion of the soul at one point into humans). John Paul II officially apologized to Galileo for the Church's poor judgment in his case. As John Paul praised Galileo's remarkable achievements, he neatly tucked science under the wing of religion: "Galileo sensed in his scientific research the presence of the Creator who, stirring in the depths of his spirit, stimulated him, anticipating and assisting his intuitions."[6] The pope describes God as the secret patron of all good scientists, inspiring their best discoveries. Science, endorsed by God and consistent with the basic tenets of theism, provides a strong foundation for arguments in support of his existence. Believers need not—indeed, should not—resort to the mere "assertion of fideistic certainties,"[7] as Polkinghorne writes. They have much better material to work with.

ASSERTION OF FIDEISTIC CERTAINTIES

As a first step in analyzing the rhetoric of faithful science, it might be helpful to raise a question related to this last quotation: in practice, how well do faithful scientists avoid the mere "assertion of fideistic certainties"? It turns out that, despite their best intentions, they cannot quite manage without them. There are moments in all three books that present a truth more by fiat than delineated argument.

Even Polkinghorne, who explicitly abjures fideistic assertions, occasionally finds them indispensable. Reflecting on the human intellect's ability to recognize the patterns of the cosmos, he writes, "I believe that the reason within and the reason without fit together because they have a common origin in the God who is the ground both of human mental experience and of the existence of the physical world of which we are a part."[8] Most of his book consists of careful scientific arguments; indeed, his explanations of quantum physics stand out for their clarity and sophistication. But here he cannot avoid the prefatory "I believe." In effect, he concedes that what follows must be considered an article of faith, not a conclusion drawn from scientific reasoning. He resorts to "I believe" a handful of other times in his book, about the soul, the resurrection, and the divinity of Christ.

Collins includes a few passages where he leaps to a definitive conclusion without supplying the intermediate reasoning. Narrating his gradual conversion from atheism, he explains how reading C. S. Lewis was steering him toward belief: "And if that were so, what kind of God would this be? Would this be a deist God who invented physics and mathematics and started the universe in motion about 14 billion years ago, then wandered off to deal with other, more important matters, as Einstein thought?"[9] It seems a plausible suggestion—and it was good enough for many Enlightenment philosophers, who, to be sure, would not have anthropomorphized God the way Collins does. But Collins simply dismisses it: "No, this God, if I was perceiving Him at all, must be a theist God, who desires some kind of relationship with those special creatures called human beings."[10] With just a shake of his head, he denies deism. Instead of offering a real explanation, he begs the question, assuming as true what was to be proved: humans are "special creatures" with an intrinsic link to God. Another example of fideistic assertion comes after Collins acknowledges, "At this point, godless materialists might be cheering. If humans evolved strictly by mutation and natural selection, who needs God to explain us? To this, I reply: I do."[11] Again, he wins the argument simply by fiat. He believes that humans are spiritually distinct from chimpanzees, despite their genetic similarities: "In my view, DNA sequence alone . . . will never explain certain special human attributes."[12] "In my view" is roughly the equivalent of Polkinghorne's "I believe."

Gingerich often resorts to some version of these prefatory qualifiers. "*To me,* belief in a final cause, a Creator-God,"[13] seems the best course. "*I am personally persuaded* that a superintelligent Creator exists beyond and within the cosmos."[14] "Personally" amounts to a kind of apology from the scientist for offering up a theological black box. "*For me,* it makes sense to suppose" that the life of Christ revealed the divine purpose of the universe.[15] Sometimes his prefatory phrases concede more frankly that a vulnerable conclusion is about to come. "*I would prefer to accept* a universe created with intention and purpose by a loving God."[16] "*It just might be*" that our divine origin accounts for altruism.[17] Gingerich ends his book by acknowledging the inevitability of fideistic assertions. "I have attempted a reasoned discourse," he says, "but perhaps I should conclude with the words of Blaise Pascal, from *Penseés* 16: 'The heart has its reasons that reason does not know.'"[18]

ROMANTIC DICTION

Faithful scientists sometimes elevate their diction to lift their subject from reason to something higher (if vaguer)—a Romantic realm governed by "the heart." As strongly as they believe in the scientific justification of theism, they feel a need to reach beyond the grasp of scientific truth. Near the end of his book, as he discusses his BioLogos initiative, Collins concedes that "BioLogos is not intended as a scientific theory. Its truth can be tested only by the spiritual logic of the heart, the mind, and the soul."[19] He links "logic" to this "heart" world, but it must be some sublime apotheosis of logic, distinct from its secular counterpart.

Occasionally the faithful scientists approach the world of the heart by infusing their arguments with references to aesthetic rather than analytical gratification. They adopt a conventional Romantic perspective that the experience of beauty trumps the experience of rational understanding. Polkinghorne contrasts two modes of experiencing music: "A scientist, speaking as a scientist, can say no more about music than that it is vibrations in the air, but speaking as a person there would surely be much more to say about the mysterious way in which a temporal succession of sounds can give us access to a timeless realm of beauty."[20] Much more dramatically, Collins narrates the climax of his conversion as an aesthetic event. He has gone for a hike in the Cascades. "As I rounded a corner and saw a beautiful and unexpected frozen waterfall, hundreds of feet high, I knew the search was over. The next morning, I knelt in the dewy grass as the sun rose and surrendered to Jesus Christ."[21] From the point of view of scientific reason, a waterfall in its predictably natural form should make no difference to arguments about belief. But Collins had set his receiver to another channel; he was listening to the voice of a new master.

Faithful scientists like to use the words "awe" and "wonder" to link their arguments with the world of the heart. Both words suggest a state of excited consciousness, similar to the way Collins felt at the waterfall, that makes reason seem drab by comparison. In his chapter on "Questions without Answers" (about purpose and teleology), Gingerich refers to the Biblical passage about the "still, small voice" that follows a series of more dramatic natural events where the voice of the Lord might have been expected. "It is that still, small voice," he writes, "arising from a sense of awe and wonder and reverence, that can point us toward some tentative insights into these questions without answers."[22] Collins uses "awe and longing" to describe moments along his path to conversion. Listening to the descant on a familiar Christmas carol "left me with a sense of unexpected awe and a longing for something I could not name. Much later, as an atheist graduate student, I surprised myself by experiencing this same sense of awe and longing, this time mixed with a particularly deep sense of grief, at the playing of the second movement of Beethoven's Third Symphony."[23] His awe always brings with it an emotional void, a longing for something unnamable that is missing from his life. The more masterful he becomes in his scientific studies, the more keenly he feels this longing.

Polkinghorne, undoubtedly the least Romantic of the faithful scientists, still uses "wonder" to describe what a scientist might feel on discovering the laws of the cosmos. The scientist receives "the reward of wonder for all the labours of his research";[24] "religious belief suggests that it is indeed the Mind of the Creator that lies behind the wonderful order of the universe."[25] Gingerich find DNA "wondrous" and our fine-tuned universe "a miracle."[26] He looks on nature with "a sense of surprise, wonder, and mystery," and he quotes Einstein for support: "The most beautiful experience we can have is the mysterious. . . . Whoever does not know it and can no longer wonder, no longer marvel, is as good as dead."[27] For faithful scientists, it is convenient to link awe and wonder with the processes and discoveries of science. They nevertheless feel the need, from time to time, for a Romantic rhetorical boost that momentarily transfigures the scientific mind and world. In their most sublime expressions of religious impulses, they welcome the messages of the heart over which reason has no jurisdiction.

APPEAL TO AUTHORITY

Gingerich's use of the Einstein quotation signals another important rhetorical gesture in the writings of faithful scientists: citation of scientific celebrities. In order to supplement the scientific arguments proper and their own inferences, they introduce comments from elite theorists that appear to support theistic positions. The citation of these authorities provides something like a secular version of scriptural evidence. Just as Biblical material comes from an elevated, indisputable source, the thoughts of scientific geniuses count as revelations beyond the capacity of ordinary humans.

Albert Einstein is the most conspicuous of these quasi-scriptural authorities. Not only has his name become synonymous with genius, but he offered quite a number of comments touching on religious questions. The closest contemporary equivalent to Einstein is Stephen Hawking, and faithful scientists have found promising material in a few of his reflections. Other theoretical physicists also enter as authorities, including Freeman Dyson, Fred Hoyle, and John Wheeler—all of them, like Einstein and Hawking, distinguished contributors to contemporary models of the cosmos. The elite among theoretical physicists provide the most value as authorities, likely for two reasons. Those who have risen to the top of the class in the arcane subjects of quantum mechanics and general relativity are presumed to be the most intelligent among us. And theoretical physics by its very nature aligns well with questions of cosmic design.

The authorities most valuable to faithful science are undoubtedly Einstein and Hawking. Although both of them can plausibly be pressed into duty to buttress theism, more thorough analysis tends to undermine the intended effects of the comments quoted by theists. Attempts to cite genius physicists as secular scripture often decay into "appeal to authority." Appeal to authority (or *argumentum ad verecundiam*) is the name given to an attractive but often defective rhetorical strategy. An authority is cited as primary evidence for a thesis, but that authority might not actually count as an expert in the relevant field; or he or she might be delivering just one opinion about a subject on which valid authorities hold differing views. In the case of physicists-turned-theologians, it is no simple matter to judge the appropriateness of scientific expertise when applied to a religious topic. To some degree, the questions and methods do not align well (do not "overlap," as Stephen Jay Gould had it),[28] but to some degree they do. The Big Bang theory, after all, emerged from physics directly into the embrace of Genesis and Christian theology. As to the second doubt about the appeal to authority, that the claim may oversimplify a complex set of opinions, here faithful scientists clearly run into trouble. Quoting someone like Einstein proves risky, because his varied comments on God and religion gratify theists and atheists in equal measure.

Francis Collins employs the appeal to authority most dexterously of the faithful scientists. His use of Einstein illustrates how the great name can serve theistic purposes. As Collins discusses the origins of the universe and ways of integrating scientific and religious ideas about cosmic fundamentals, he quotes Einstein's well-known skeptical remark about quantum mechanics: "God does not play dice."[29] The point here is not to challenge or affirm the validity of probability and uncertainty, key quantum concepts on which Collins takes no stand. What matters is that Einstein invoked God in a way that sounds perfectly in sync with Judeo-Christian theism. A little later Collins classifies Einstein as a deist, akin to the intellectual theists of the Enlightenment who saw God as a remote watchmaker: "Deists like Einstein, who view God as having started the whole process but then paying no attention to subsequent developments, are generally comfortable with recent conclusions of physics and cosmology."[30] Later, Collins deploys another Einstein remark to keynote his climactic argument that science needs religion to probe the deepest truths: "Even Albert Einstein saw the poverty of a purely naturalistic worldview. Choosing his words carefully, he wrote, 'Science without religion is lame, religion without science is blind.'"[31] Collins gives us an Einstein fully invested in science who nevertheless seems religious enough to serve as an ally in the battle against atheism.

Other theists, whether scientists or not, have been delighted to find evidence that the genius of modern physics agreed with them about God. They draw many supportive remarks—including those mentioned by Collins—from Max Jammer's *Einstein and Religion*, the most comprehensive treatment of the subject. Jammer was Einstein's colleague and friend. But several of the remarks in Jammer most attractive to theists are more complicated in full context than they appear when extracted. One such remark has Einstein describing himself as religious: "Behind all the discernible concat-enations, there remains something subtle, intangible, and inexpli-cable. Veneration for this force is my religion. To that extent, I am in point of fact religious."[32] Einstein's bold declaration makes more sense in its social context. He was at a dinner party that included a wit named Alfred Kerr, who (according to Jammer) made "the sub-ject of God a special butt for his derision."[33] When someone told Kerr that Einstein might be offended by his comments, Kerr refused to believe it. He approached Einstein and insisted that the great sci-entist deny the silly rumor that he was religious. Einstein's reply shows his irritation over Kerr's arrogance; he was obviously happy to contradict the man. This context does not invalidate what he said, but it does help explain the unusual forcefulness of his tone.

Evidently Einstein had little patience for ideologues on either side of the debate. Theists like to quote his criticism of athe-ists: "Then there are the fanatical atheists whose intolerance is of the same kind as the intolerance of the religious fanatics and comes from the same source."[34] He wrote this in reaction to atheists' crit-icism of his 1940 essay on "Science and Religion." But in the same letter he was even more pointed in his criticism of the way believers read his essay: "I was barked at by numerous dogs who are earn-ing their food guarding ignorance and superstition for the benefit of those who profit from it."[35] Einstein had little sympathy for institu-tional religion. Jammer notes that he "refused to become barmitzva-hed," "never attended religious service," and "his last wish was not to be buried in the Jewish tradition."[36]

In another quotation useful to faithful science, Einstein links science with spirituality: "Every scientist becomes convinced that the laws of nature manifest the existence of a spirit vastly superior to that of men."[37] This nugget comes from a letter he wrote in reply to Phyllis, a sixth grader attending Sunday school at the Riverside

Church. Phyllis had asked him whether scientists pray and what they pray for. Einstein must have inferred that she was anxious about the issue, and he replied in a way that would not disturb her faith. Even so, at the end of the letter he adds a little jab at "naïve" belief: "The pursuit of science leads therefore to a religious feeling of a special kind, which differs from the religiosity of more naïve people."[38]

The key to understanding Einstein's religious views lies in the philosophy of Spinoza. According to Jammer, Einstein "declared that his 'views are near to those of Spinoza.'. . . Spinoza's *Ethics* had been read repeatedly by Einstein."[39] In 1929, when asked by a rabbi whether he believed in God, Einstein replied, "I believe in Spinoza's God."[40] Spinoza emphatically repudiated the idea of a personal God. Einstein did likewise, throughout his life. Naïve believers worship a deity imagined as having human characteristics and motivations, someone attentive to what we do and ready to judge good and bad behavior. Spinoza thought this was nonsense. He refers to God as simply the uncaused cause of the natural world. In the most notorious sentence from the *Ethics*, Spinoza called this fundamental entity "God, or Nature" (*"Deus, sive Natura"*): "That eternal and infinite being we call God, or Nature, acts from the same necessity from which he exists."[41] Traditional theists may find just enough here to tolerate Spinoza, but *"Deus, sive Natura"* so alarmed his friends that they deleted *"sive Natura"* from the Dutch translation published after his death. Contemporary philosophers tend to see Spinoza as a sort of proto-atheist, however carefully he hedged the concept of God. Even in his own time, his ideas were condemned by the Jewish community to the point of excommunication.

Einstein, like his mentor Spinoza, is hard to label with the usual religious descriptors. He once said, "I am not an atheist"—and although Richard Dawkins claims him as one of his tribe, Einstein clearly did not like the implications of that label.[42] Einstein also said,

"I don't think I can call myself a pantheist."[43] Spinoza has often been classified as a pantheist by historians of philosophy, but like Einstein, he would probably be uncomfortable with the warm and fuzzy sentiments associated with pantheism. Perhaps the least controversial label for both Spinoza and Einstein would be deist. Deism amounts to a colder version of pantheism, perilously close to but distinct from atheism. Collins uses the label "deist" for Einstein—although if this were a perfect fit, Einstein would probably have embraced it and left no doubt. Einstein's religious ideas were so fine grained that they slipped through every filter.

The contemporary Einstein, Stephen Hawking, is not so hard to label. As Chris Matyszczyk noted on cnet, Hawking said straight out in a 2014 interview, "I'm an atheist."[44] Hawking had been asked by the interviewer about two references to God in A Brief History of Time. Both of these references have been put to good use by faithful science. Collins quotes Hawking dramatically to introduce his own notion of the "languages of God": "In the final sentences of A Brief History of Time, Stephen Hawking (not generally given to metaphysical musings) says, 'If we find the answer to that [why the universe exists], it would be the ultimate triumph of human reason—for then we would know the mind of God.' Are these mathematical descriptions of reality signposts to some greater intelligence? Is mathematics, like DNA, another language of God?"[45] Certainly Collins can be excused for embracing Hawking as a fellow believer, but Hawking's 2014 clarification ruins the effect. Hawking directly addressed this passage in 2014. "Before we understand science," he told the interviewer, "it is natural to believe that God created the universe. But now science offers a more convincing explanation. What I meant by 'we would know the mind of God' is, we would know everything that God would know, if there were a God, which there isn't. I'm an atheist."[46]

The other plausibly theistic passage from *A Brief History of Time* sounds even more promising. As Collins mounts his argument that the "fine tuning" of the universe indicates a divine purpose to create a universe where humans thrive, he quotes Hawking as an expert witness: "Going even further, in *A Brief History of Time* Hawking states: 'It would be very difficult to explain why the universe should have begun in just this way, except as the act of a God who intended to create beings like us.'"[47] Again, the quotation fits perfectly with the ideas of faithful science—but only as it sits extracted from context. The sentence comes from Hawking's chapter on "The Origin and Fate of the Universe." In this chapter, he addresses a number of models for how the universe began. One of these models is the "hot big bang theory," which, if true, would seem to imply that only a set of rare, perfect conditions allowed our universe to come into being. It is in this context that Hawking writes about the "act of a God." Unfortunately for faithful science, Hawking's comment about God is purely hypothetical and is swept aside to make room for better alternatives. The "act of God" reasoning depends on a hot big bang model being correct, but other models have become more attractive (especially those connected with Guth's "inflationary" theory). Hawking devotes much of the chapter to other models, including his own "no boundary" approach. He ends with a passage that will never appear in faithful science: "So long as the universe had a beginning, we could suppose it had a creator. But if the universe is really completely self-contained, having no boundary or edge, it would have neither beginning nor end: it would simply be. What place, then, for a creator?"[48]

Those who read and write faithful science can still find ways to restore the value of Einstein and Hawking, even as the two geniuses are unmasked as Spinozist and atheist. Einstein's comments give ample interpretive room for those who seek some sort of spiritual supplement to materialism. And Hawking certainly brings up God a lot for a resolute atheist; perhaps he will one day see the light. There is nothing theists can do, however, about Steven Weinberg. Weinberg, considered by many to be the preeminent particle physicist of our time, dismissed religious hopes with this sobering demystification: "It is almost irresistible for humans to believe that we have some special relation to the universe, that human life is not just a farcical outcome of a chain of accidents, . . . but that we were somehow built in from the beginning. . . . It is very hard for us to realize that [Earth] is just a tiny part of an overwhelmingly hostile universe. . . . The more the universe seems comprehensible, the more it also seems pointless."[49]

Weinberg's "pointless" remark has been quoted, bravely, by a few of the faithful scientists, including Gingerich. Gingerich wrote about how he once invited Weinberg and Polkinghorne, both of them elite particle physicists, for a public debate about whether the universe shows signs of design. Polkinghorne argued for design, while Weinberg stood by pointlessness. Weinberg haunts faithful science as Polkinghorne's atheist doppelgänger. If scientific knowledge can really be said to harmonize with theistic teleology—as Gingerich, Polkinghorne, and Collins all maintain—it is unsettling to see a scientist so accomplished in physics and so bleak in his assessment of our place in the cosmos.

INFELICITOUS MIX OF DISCOURSES

Apart from all these rhetorical supplements to, and deviations from, the science itself, the main business of scientific argument often complicates the messages of faithful science. In their efforts to demonstrate the harmonious relationship between science and religion, they sometimes weaken their cause with an infelicitous mix of the two modes of discourse. The effort to elucidate faith through science sometimes fails to persuade—often due either to a dubious analogy or to mismatched explanatory models.

One interesting example comes as Polkinghorne mixes Christian theology with mathematics. He believes that "creation is intrinsically a two-step process": the "old creation," which we recognize in the natural processes of life, decay, and death, will eventually be replaced by the "new creation in which the divine presence is no longer veiled from view."[50] Christ's resurrection offers a glimpse of the new creation. "The tomb was empty," he explains, "because the matter of his dead corpse had been transformed into the 'matter' of his risen and glorified body. The old and new creations now exist 'alongside' each other in different dimensions (an idea perhaps easier for mathematicians than for most people to visualize)."[51] Here the modern physicist mixes awkwardly with the traditional cleric. Polkinghorne's reflections on the resurrection come straight from the pulpit; he even adds a dutiful scriptural citation from Colossians. Then he cannot resist an analogy drawn from the mathematics of category theory. The analogy juxtaposes sublime religious mystery with the most precise tool of human reason. Does a mathematical model do any good at all to clarify the outlandishly supernatural idea of the resurrection? To some extent, Polkinghorne is bragging with the analogy, reminding us of his elite intellectual status. But the mix of math and miracle seems clumsy. It is unlikely either to convert a secular mathematician or to improve the faith of a believer. A similarly awkward moment arises as Polkinghorne discusses the problematic relationship between human free will and divine providence.

In the discussion of providential agency, different people have laid stress on different aspects of intrinsic unpredictability in their attempts to speak of the "causal joint" by which this action might be effected. Some have emphasised quantum physics, supposing that God may act principally by determining all—or perhaps only some of the most potentially significant—quantum events, while keeping this carefully hidden by ensuring that the overall statistical distribution of outcomes remains compatible with the laws of quantum mechanics, for these too are expressions of the Creator's will.[52]

Again, Polkinghorne's impressive grasp of physics creates more dissonance than harmony between the worlds of quantum mechanics and theology. The idea of God determining quantum events one by one offers an updated version of deism, even colder and less inspiring than Paley's watchmaker. Polkinghorne's speculation about the creator has him altering quantum results, in effect rigging the odds, all the while "keeping this carefully hidden." Here is God playing dice, as Einstein complained, but this time with loaded dice.

Collins finds trouble when he tries to wed physics with Genesis. "The Big Bang cries out for a divine explanation. I cannot see how nature could have created itself. Only a supernatural force that is outside of space and time could have done that."[53] He presents the evidence from physics as if it amounted to a proof of God, but the argument has two conspicuous weaknesses. Physics indicates that what we know as time and space only began with the Big Bang. "Outside of space and time" therefore invites a materialist explanation just as easily as a supernatural one. What makes Collins even more vulnerable is his assertion, "I cannot see how nature could have created itself." Physicists like Lawrence Krauss have offered plausible theories of how the fundamental quantum conditions inherent in nature can generate "something" from "nothing." This is not to say that Krauss has securely proved his case against all theist objections; but because physics provides reasonable alternatives to supernatural explanations, the use of science to confirm faith proves unreliable. Indeed, a curious believer might find his faith challenged by the autonomy and resourcefulness of scientific explanation. Bringing physics to bear on theology might do more harm than good for the cause of faithful science.

All of the faithful scientists recognize a problem called "God of the gaps." If believers base their faith on a supernatural explanation of something that science cannot account for—a gap in science, so to speak—they risk losing faith when science fills the gap with a perfectly natural explanation. God is no longer needed. ("I had no need of that hypothesis," as Laplace supposedly replied when Napoleon asked how a creator entered his theories.) Collins's argument about the Big Bang falters as the physics of quantum "nothingness" increasingly makes some headway. He invites a similar "God of the gaps" problem when he claims that human uniqueness strongly supports theism: "Humans are unique in ways that defy evolutionary explanation," including our moral standards and our universal "search for God."[54] This puts him on shaky ground. Evolutionary explanations have been among the most resourceful and successful in recent science, and it is dangerous to assume that any natural phenomenon will always "defy evolutionary explanation." Atheists like Richard Dawkins have no trouble at all offering evolutionary theories for moral codes and religious inclinations.

The most persuasive faithful scientists all recognize the validity of evolution and its underlying biological processes. Sometimes, however, evolution and religion make strange bedfellows. Gingerich raises the question of genetic mutation as a problem at the intersection of materialist and supernatural arguments. Mutation has implications of randomness and chaos that the faithful may find troubling. He rejects the "Intelligent Design" movement as insufficiently attentive to science, in part because they cannot account for the fact that "most mutations are disasters." Gingerich wants to suggest that "perhaps some inspired few [mutations] are not," although he acknowledges that many colleagues might balk at the notion of an "inspired mutation."[55] Collins, human genome specialist, unintentionally sends a mixed message about DNA and faith. He celebrates DNA as a "language of God,"[56] but he also refers to "glitches in the genome" that cause diseases and Down syndrome.[57] Someone looking for confirmation of theism might have difficulty recognizing the glitchy, cancer-filled world of DNA as the language of a benevolent God.

DIFFICULTIES OF THEODICY

Indeed, the greatest challenge for faithful science is the age-old problem of theodicy: to justify the presence of so much evil and suffering in a universe overseen by a benevolent God. Polkinghorne engages the problem with the most explicit theological arguments. Polkinghorne's God is "kenotic," which means that he has chosen to empty or limit himself so that natural creation can pursue its own free development. God wants humans to exercise free will. The free will aspect of theodicy, which explains evil as the unfortunate result of poor human choices, has a long history and makes good enough sense (as along as one brackets the tricky philosophical problems of free will and determinacy). The more difficult explanation relates not to humans, but to things—like cancerous mutations. This is where faithful science struggles to reconcile evolutionary microbiology with the idea of a benevolent creator. "Genetic mutation of germ cells has driven the evolution of life," writes Polkinghorne, "but when somatic (body) cells mutate they can become malignant.

The existence of cancer is part of the shadow side of evolution."[58] Later, he says of helpful and malignant mutations, "One cannot have one without the other."[59] Polkinghorne refers to the "free process" of nature that a kenotic God has unleashed.

Only the most faithful cancer patients, I suspect, will find the free process argument compelling. For agnostics or those with wavering faith, it will likely do two things to steer them away from theism. First, it may persuade them that science is the only truly significant agent in this process; only research oncologists, after all, could someday rid evolutionary mutations of their shadow side. (The "free process" argument certainly allows for this eventuality.) And those whose faith depends on a benevolent God may find it hard to understand that such a God would supervise a natural system so glitch-ridden that it causes gratuitous suffering. Although Polkinghorne explains the kenotic thesis carefully, it clashes with certain rhetorical elements of his book that emphasize the "rational beauty" of the universe: "Science has disclosed to us a world which, in its rational transparency and beauty, is shot through with signs of mind, and religious belief suggests that it is indeed the Mind of the Creator that lies behind the wonderful order of the universe."[60] He selects only those features we recognize as beautiful and orderly to represent the whole universe; this amounts to a metonymic reduction, deployed to improve the logic of theodicy. As much as Polkinghorne wishes to usher in science as a welcome partner to theology, the cancerous mutations discovered by science bedevil the "wonderful order" posited by believers.

Both Gingerich and Collins turn to the old trope of pathopoeia as they address the problem of evil and suffering. Devout but not ordained, they seem less engaged with Polkinghorne's abstract theological arguments; they find it more compelling to present emotionally charged memories of personal suffering. In these instances of pathopoeia, the implied message goes something like this: if I, who have suffered in a way that seems to defy justification, can still believe in a benevolent God, then so should you. The trope turns the logic of suffering against itself. Rationally we should not believe in God's benevolence, but deep emotions trump reason and invite faith-filled transcendence.

Gingerich's pathopoeia comes in climactic position near the end of his book: "When I was seventeen, my only brother, biking at dusk on his paper route, was struck by a car, and a few hours later he breathed his last in the hospital. A quarter of a century later, in one of the last entries in his diary, my father, a man of deep faith, wrote that he could still not understand how God had allowed his young son to die."[61] Details of his narrative sharpen the emotional impact. His "only brother," doing his innocent job responsibly, "breathed his last"; his father, still distraught after so many years, made a painful diary entry as he approached his own death. Like his father, Gingerich is "a man of deep faith" who acknowledges that it can be hard to believe in God's benevolence. He exposes his emotions so that any suffering reader might find strength in the fact that this man has not lost his faith. Still, a hint of dissonance emerges at the end of this pathopoeia. To some extent, Gingerich the scientist rebels against Gingerich the believer: "Ours is a world of love and ecstatic joy, but also a world of suffering and excruciating pain. . . . Why creation is this way is perhaps the most unanswerable question of all."[62] The believer accepts God's creation just as he finds it, but the scientist seems impatient for a rational answer.

Even more poignant is a moment of pathopoeia from Collins's book. He tells the story of a college student preparing for a medical career who was raped in her apartment by a violent intruder. The rapist was never caught. Collins begins the next paragraph, "That young woman was my daughter."[63] The suspended identification of the victim dramatically amplifies the pathos. He sets out the obvious questions that challenged the faith of a suffering father. "Never did I more passionately wish that God would have intervened somehow to stop this terrible crime. . . . Why didn't he cause the perpetrator to be struck with a bolt of lightning, or at least a pang of conscience? Why didn't He put an invisible shield around my daughter to protect her?"[64] After frankly expressing all his doubts, Collins does his best to provide a faithful answer. He summarizes the argument about God empowering human free will. He adds that the experience of suffering, while terrible in the moment, may enrich our humanity, move us beyond self-centered complacency, and help us learn the difficult virtue of forgiveness.

As sensible as these faithful arguments seem, Collins, like Gingerich, allows the scientist to rebel a little against the believer. "In my case I can see, albeit dimly, that my daughter's rape was a challenge for me to try to learn the real meaning of forgiveness in a terribly wrenching circumstance. In complete honesty, I am still working on that."[65] He admits that the truths of faith can be glimpsed only "dimly"—through a glass darkly, as it were. The genetic scientist would prefer a bright and definitive anatomy of God's design, every bit as satisfying as the fully articulated human genome. This is the promise implied in Collins's subtitle: "A Scientist Presents Evidence for Belief." In the end, however, this scientist "is still working on that." Scientific reason, all by itself, can neither confirm faith nor convert the faithless.

Christians and Adversaries in the Evolving *Norton Anthology of English Literature*

Old Time Religion and the New Academic Market

Contemporary scholars of English literature face an important but overlooked entanglement of religious and secular interests. Several core works in the English literary canon take Christian values for granted, and some of the most influential writers considered it their primary purpose to articulate Christian truth. Many literature professors in decades past who shared the religious convictions of canonical Christian writers had no qualms about embracing those convictions in their interpretive work. Facing new cultural conditions and an evolving academic literary market, professors in the twenty-first century have gradually adapted. Those who edit, interpret, and teach such works as *The Faerie Queene* and *Paradise Lost* now must negotiate a complicated entanglement of old-fashioned Christian convictions, still the foundation of those works, and a new literary secularism premised on belief-neutral toleration.

The Norton Anthology of English Literature presents a very helpful body of evidence for the study of these evolving literary perspectives.

Editors' notes in the early editions tend to reflect the viewpoint of Christian insiders; later editions alter notes to accommodate a more secular paradigm and a greater sensitivity to religious diversity. By tracking notes about three kinds of Christian adversary, we can analyze in detail how the old and new interact. In each case, something old—Robert Adams's frankly Christian repudiation of Milton's Satan; Christian antipathy to the Islamic world; and heterocentric sexual values—entangles with something new: a secular sympathy for Satan; sensitivity to Islamic history and interests; and queer-friendly sexual pluralism.

ANNOTATION AND ADAPTATION

Across nine editions and fifty turbulent years of literary studies, *Norton* has maintained a consistent if mildly contradictory philosophy of annotation. On the one hand, writes founding editor M. H. Abrams, editorial interventions should be informative rather than interpretive and provide the "least impediment to the normal flow of reading."[1] Headnotes and footnotes aim to be "as simple and lucid as possible,"[2] with editors making "a special effort to minimize commentary that is interpretive rather than, in a very limited sense, explanatory."[3] Stephen Greenblatt's preface to the 2006 edition, the first in which he fully replaced Abrams as general editor, reiterates Abrams's preference for notes that deliver plain information: "Period introductions, headnotes, and annotation are designed to enhance students' reading and, without imposing an interpretation, to give students the information they need to understand each text."[4] And in the newly published ninth edition, Greenblatt sharpens his remark about "imposing an interpretation": the anthology "is not a place for the display of pedantry, the pushing of cherished theories, or the promotion of a narrow ideological agenda."[5] However much social conservatives have complained about an ideologically tilted English classroom, *Norton* separates itself from the fuss of culture wars by defining its core annotative purpose as explanatory rather than interpretive.

On the other hand, both Abrams and Greenblatt recognize that they cannot rule out interpretive notes altogether. Abrams negotiates a compromise that will allow interpretive notes in certain cases, to give students help with difficult texts not addressed during class discussions. "In selected instances," he writes in the preface to the third edition, "editorial headnotes or footnotes briefly indicate possible interpretations of a difficult work or passage. The reason for this procedure is a practical one. The anthology includes some of the most complex and problematic writings in the language, and the normal procedure in teaching the course is to assign a number of texts which there is no time to discuss adequately."[6] Although he wants the anthology only minimally dressed with such acts of editorial interpretation—"Our endeavor is to provide a necessary modicum of guidance to the student, but in a fashion that simply opens out possibilities for his independent judgment"—Abrams's self-sufficient, stand-alone book must include some material that steers students toward "the best that has been thought and said about literature."[7]

Later editions will drop the Matthew Arnold echo, which sounded a little old-fashioned even back in 1962. Both Abrams and Greenblatt recognize that there are theoretical as well as practical complications surrounding the selection of "the best" in literary interpretation. From the beginning, Abrams distinguished between scholarship and criticism; in scholarship, notably the realm of textual archaeology, quality and progress are more easily judged than in interpretive criticism. In one preface, for example, Abrams comments, "The changes in this edition are in line with recent scholarly discoveries and important shifts in critical interests."[8] Scholarship yields "discoveries," but criticism rests on the less scientific foundation of "shifting interests." Greenblatt in his prefaces pays tribute to Abrams's methods and preserves his terminology: both presiding editors understand "that new scholarly discoveries and the shifting interests of readers constantly alter the landscape of literary history."[9]

As the landscape of literary history showed signs of significant alteration in the late twentieth century, *Norton* editors reacted anxiously to the threat posed by an upcoming rival, *The Longman Anthology of British Literature* (1999). The *Longman* promised better coverage of historical contexts and greater inclusion of women writers. It looked to be a more formidable competitor than an earlier challenger, *The Oxford Anthology of English Literature* (1974), which never made much headway against the market heavyweight. Editor David Damrosch argued that his *Longman* better registered the "shifting currents" of contemporary society: in emphasizing the "variety of British linguistic and literary culture, the *Longman Anthology* is reflecting a current waning of the melting-pot idea of culture" in Britain, along with "the rise of 'multiculturalism' in North America."[10] In the months leading up to the seventh edition, *Norton* hustled to make revisions to keep it viable against *Longman*: to evolve, in other words, in response to changes in the environment.

The famous anthology leaves the equivalent of a fossil record in editors' explanatory notes. While *Norton* editors usually heed Abrams's preference for strictly informational annotation, even such plain notes can quietly reflect something more than a neutral interpretive perspective; eventually such notes may need revision to thrive in an altered literary environment. Notes connected either explicitly or implicitly with religious perspectives are particularly useful for the study of this process. Here the boundaries between information and interpretation are not always so clear. Especially in the earlier periods, the anthology aims to guide readers through the Christian ideas embedded in works like *The Faerie Queene* and *Paradise Lost*, all the while attempting to maintain a tolerant, pluralistic separation between church and textbook. Sometimes, however, editors' assumptions and conceptual habits threaten this separation and possibly jeopardize the book's marketability to the broadest possible audience.

Annotations about three Christian adversaries leave an intriguing fossil record. The very name of Satan defines him as ur-adversary in the Judeo-Christian tradition, and Robert Adams treats him with unmitigated scorn. Adams's frankly Christian perspective makes his notes about Milton's Satan among the most entertaining in *Norton*, but also among the most vulnerable to revision. The adversarial relationship between Christianity and the Islamic world has deep historical roots and poses much subtler challenges for annotators. Christian-Muslim opposition entered English literature in the context of the Crusades—whether as contemporary context, for Chaucer, or as historical paradigm, for Spenser—and gained new relevance with the American wars of the late twentieth and early twenty-first centuries, as well as the fatwa declared against Salman Rushdie. Finally, the case of poet and priest Gerard Manley Hopkins poses a delicate problem for annotators. Hopkins battled against hard-to-define adversaries as he struggled to maintain his faith and equanimity. What information should the evolving anthology offer about Hopkins's internal adversaries? Should hints of queer sexuality be included or excluded as background information? The stigma attached to same-sex attraction, of course, was not exclusively a Christian or a religious phenomenon: until 1973, mainstream psychiatry classified it as a disorder. But many Christian communities have viewed queer sexuality as a particular threat to virtue, and some continue to treat it as an adversary, even in the altered sexual landscape of the twenty-first century.

In each of these cases, *Norton* adaptations follow a recognizable pattern. Earlier annotations regarding the adversaries are more likely to show signs of a Christian insider's perspective. Over time, editors gradually remove or remake such notes as the anthology sharpens its liberal tolerance and aims for belief-neutral annotation; usually the newer notes express increasing sympathy for the adversaries. As *Norton* adapts to reflect the shifting interests and assumptions of the contemporary literary community, it makes the anthology more marketable, surely, and for many readers the changes amount to something more profound: it may feel as if the textbook is making intellectual progress away from outdated parochialism. But "progress" is a contested term—and not a concept that meshes comfortably with antifoundationalism, still a strong influence within contemporary literary studies. Some literary scholars have joined religious and political theorists in raising doubts about simple models of liberal, secular progress. In a recent essay about Astell and Shaftesbury, for example, David Alvarez cites Wendy Brown's call "to puncture the aura of pure goodness that contemporary invocations of tolerance carry," and he concludes, "I am not, of course, arguing against religious tolerance. . . . But scholarly enthusiasm for identifying with and reproducing Shaftesbury's construction of reason and a tolerant subject has contributed to an ongoing blindness about the cultural specificity and political force of liberal religious tolerance."[11] In the case of the evolving *Norton*, increasingly tolerant, secular annotations have altered the anthology's relationship to Christianity, but they are not belief-neutral in any simple sense; nor have they managed to circumvent, let alone resolve, interpretive conflicts that have always complicated the overlapping discourses of literature and religion.

SATAN

Robert Adams's notes to *Paradise Lost* offer some of the boldest interpretive assertions in *Norton*, many of which proceed from a Christian insider's perspective. In his headnote to the poem, he composes this stirring homiletic climax: "Expelled from Eden, our first 'grand parents' pick up the burdens of humanity as we know them, sustained by a faith which we also know, and go forth to seek a blessing which we do not know yet. They are to become wayfaring, warfaring Christians, like John Milton; and in this condition, with its weaknesses and strivings and defeats, there is a glory that no devil can understand."[12] Adams draws all his academic readers into a community of intelligent Christians—"sustained by a faith which we also know"—and emphasizes the spiritual condition they share with Milton, for all the cultural differences separating them across the centuries. His headnote survives four decades of *Norton* revisions, until the seventh edition (2000) deletes it for good. Even the fifth edition (1986), with a new team of coeditors for each period and widespread rewriting of notes, did not tamper with it. This fact might seem surprising, given the tendency in *Norton* to steer away from such interpretive assertions. But the other editors must have been reluctant to excise such an eloquent and heartfelt expression of faith.

Adams's notes to *Paradise Lost* show little sympathy for Satan and for the Romantic interpretive approach that makes the epic's adversary its true hero. Adams begins his headnote by conceding Satan's superficial appeal and warning readers not to be misled: "While we are getting acclimated to the Miltonic world, there is no reason to hold back our sympathy for Satan, nor admiration for his heroic energy. It is energy in a bad cause, clearly; but it is energy, it is heroically exercised, and there is as yet no source of virtuous power to oppose or offset it." Soon enough, however, intelligent readers will recognize that "Satan is no longer a glamorous underdog, fighting his adventurous way through the universe against enormous odds; he is a menacing vulture, a cormorant, a toad, a snake. He is not only dangerous, he is dull."[13] One cannot help but admire Adams's rich prose, robust with conviction, which survives nearly forty years of pruning by editors wary of giving offense. But in the seventh edition Barbara K. Lewalski will rewrite the headnote entirely and present a much more balanced interpretive synopsis.

Some of Adams's sharp, opinionated footnotes about Satan needed tweaking much earlier. For example, in the first edition, Adams provides a footnote to this passage from book 9, as Satan sees Eve and momentarily loses his motivation:

That space the evil one abstracted stood
From his own evil, and for the time remained
Stupidly good,[9] of enmity disarmed,
Of guile, of hate, of envy, of revenge (9.463–66).
[9] Without his evil, Satan (like many wicked people) is quite dull and ordinary.[14]

Adams's footnote is deliciously extravagant. Presumably he wants to help readers understand the unusual phrase "stupidly good," but his note veers away from that task to insult Satan. Again, Adams's moral decisiveness is charming—he sums up "wicked people" in a single stroke—but the footnote does not do justice to Satan's complexity here. After all, in this moment Satan shows his residual, unconscious good nature, not his wickedness. Nor is the note helpful with the word "stupidly," which Milton uses in the obsolete sense, "in consequence of stupefaction" (*OED*). By the third edition, Adams has annexed a little help with "stupidly": "Without his evil, Satan (like many wicked people) is quite dull and ordinary. But at the moment he is stunned."[15] The note now consists of two messages awkwardly stitched together. Adams preserves his high-handed putdown of wicked people, but he grudgingly tacks on a plainer gloss of the primary meaning of "stupidly." This iteration of the footnote has a curious duplicity: it explains that Satan is wickedly dull, pauses, and then implies that he is actually rather interesting in this moment of uncharacteristic distraction. The fifth edition deletes the whole remark about wicked people and replaces it with a gloss as well as a nod to Satan's complexity: "I.e., he is momentarily stunned into a kind of vacant goodness."[16] In the seventh edition, Lewalski reduces the footnote to a marginal gloss: "good because stupefied."[17] No trace of judgment remains about either Satan or wickedness in general.

Another telling example of adaptation comes in Adams's footnote to one of Satan's early speeches:

> Be it so, since he
> Who now is sovereign can dispose and bid
> What shall be right: farthest from him is best,
> Whom reason hath equaled, force hath made supreme
> Above his equals[1] (1.245–49).
>
> [1] Satan likes to think that by "reason" he is God's equal; this only shows how far he is from "right reason."[18]

The first clause of his footnote more or less paraphrases the passage (helpful here because of Milton's tricky syntax); the second delivers a pious condemnation of Satan. For the third edition, Adams adds an explanation of the term "right reason": "that is, the reason directed and corrected by a proper sense of religious values."[19] This new information slightly diminishes the Christian assertiveness of the first edition. Because he now must explain what "right reason" means, to some degree he shifts its status from a timeless concept anyone should recognize to a period concept deployed by Milton. Adams's forceful judgment of Satan remains, but its philosophical core has been contextualized for modern students who might not share his Christian foundation. The seventh edition deletes the footnote and puts nothing in its place, letting students judge for themselves the merits of Satan's reasoning.

The seventh edition is not shy about offering interpretive cues, to be sure: Lewalski deletes Adams's most assertively Christian notes but replaces them with other interpretive gestures. In the new headnote to *Paradise Lost*, for example, she removes his climactic remarks about "wayfaring, warfaring Christians" to make room for ideas about gender complexities surrounding the character of Eve. Lewalski now refers to "the fullness and complexity of Eve's character,"[20] whereas Adams had included dismissive notes about "Eve's fatal foolishness."[21] Lewalski also describes a Satan who sounds much more attractive than Adams's version. She respects the Romantic reading—"For some readers, Satan has been the true hero of the poem"—and she suggests that Milton's affiliation with radical politics has influenced his depiction of Satan: "The great themes of *Paradise Lost* are intimately linked to the political questions at stake in the English Revolution and Restoration, but the connection is by no means simple or straightforward. This is a poem in which Satan leads a revolution against an absolute monarch and in which questions of tyranny, servitude, and liberty are debated in a Parliament in Hell."[22] At roughly the same time, *Norton*'s new competitor, the *Longman*, was investing Satan with "all the psychological complexity and verbal grandeur of a tragic hero."[23] Clearly Adams's "wicked, dull" adversary would not do for turn-of-the-century classrooms.

As tempting as it might seem to call these changes "progress," surely that term would be misleading. Lewalski's notes about Satan simply reflect a more contemporary set of academic literary interests and a cooler, cautious attitude about Christian beliefs. Adams interpreted Satan from the perspective of a decisive Christian, someone who seemed to prefer the passionate faith of earlier ages to the blander reasonableness of modernity. Indeed, when Adams wrote his headnote about John Locke, he betrayed a lack of enthusiasm for Locke's invention of modern deism. "What was left of Christianity when one got rid of all its 'unreasonable' elements," Adams writes, "was a cool, general, undemanding creed, which did not commit one to much more than a belief in the existence of God."[24] Adams's criticism of Locke comes through subtly with the faint praise of "cool" and "undemanding." He later situated Locke with Isaac Newton as "termini" at the border between the Renaissance and the Age of Reason: "They are indeed massive termini who can be seen as marking the end of the Renaissance and the onset of what we call (not without gathering reservations) the modern world."[25] *Norton* later deleted Adams's elegiac parenthetical remark about the disappointments of modernity, just as it let his grandly old-fashioned notes about Satan go extinct.

ISLAM

Norton's notes relating to the Islamic world convey interpretive positions much more subtly than did Adams's notes about Satan. When, for example, E. Talbot Donaldson provides a footnote explaining battle references in Chaucer's portrait of the Knight (General Prologue to *The Canterbury Tales*), the information he offers seems straightforward. Chaucer's narrator praises the Knight for fighting battles across "Cristendom and hethenesse." Donaldson explains the historical background: "The Knight has taken part in campaigns fought against all three groups of pagans who threatened Europe during the 14th century: the Moslems in the Near East, from whom Alexandria was seized after a famous siege; the northern barbarians in Prussia, Lithuania, and Russia; and the Moors in North Africa."[26] As plain as it appears, the footnote will eventually need adaptation for an era newly sensitized to wars dividing Christians and Muslims. Donaldson's note survives intact through the first six editions, and even the broadly revised seventh edition merely adds one word: instead of "pagans who threatened Europe," it reads, "pagans who threatened Christian Europe."[27] Christianity must now be registered along with other religious cultures, no longer tacitly identical with Europe.

More striking changes come with the eighth edition (2006), the first to appear after 9/11 and ensuing wars. Editors Alfred David and James Simpson give a different picture of the battle for Alexandria, which Donaldson had described as "a famous siege": "The capture of Alexandria in Egypt (1365) was considered a famous victory, although the Crusaders abandoned the city after a week of looting."[28] The new note turns knights into looters and questions the primary motives for their battles. Chaucer scholars had been raising doubts about the Knight for some time—most elaborately in Terry Jones's *Chaucer's Knight: The Portrait of a Medieval Mercenary*, published in 1980—but this was the first time *Norton* had registered the problem. Donaldson's earlier note had given accurate if limited information. The new editors want to ensure that contemporary students recognize a darker side to supposed Christian heroes. In the same footnote, they also mention "the Teutonic Order of Knights" who battled "on the shores of the Baltic Sea in northern Europe against the Eastern Orthodox Church."[29] Crusaders' adversaries now include not only Muslims but Christian communities, a fact that further complicates the religious background to the Knight's battles. Donaldson had made note of these combatants but under the general heading of "three groups of pagans who threatened Europe."

It was the dangerous competitor *Longman* that first referred to "14th-century Crusades against both Moslems and Eastern Orthodox Christians," which may have prompted the *Norton*'s revision.[30] A new competitor, *The Broadview Anthology of British Literature* (2006), goes even further in raising questions of Christian prejudice. *Broadview* notes that the Man of Law is "hostile to Islam" and suggests that Chaucer may have harbored unpleasant prejudices against both Muslims and Jews.[31] *Broadview* even includes "The Prioress' Tale" with its uncomfortable anti-Semitic elements. To date, *Norton* has not attached the stigma of anti-Muslim or anti-Semitic to Chaucer, although beginning with the eighth edition, the headnote on Margery Kempe refers to her "anti-Semitic reflex";[32] and in the twentieth-century volume of that same edition, the editors for the first time call attention to T. S. Eliot's "anti-Semitic remarks."[33]

Notes to Spenser's *The Faerie Queene* show a similar process of adaptation regarding Christian-Muslim conflict. Book 1 of *The Faerie Queene* pits Christian hero Redcrosse against a trio of "Saracen" brothers: Sansfoy, Sansloy, and Sansjoy. Although Spenser's use of "Saracen" marks them as Muslim in a literary world still defined by the Crusades, an early note about Sansfoy represses the historical connection. When Sansfoy first appears, editor Hallett Smith glosses him with allegory based on simple translation: "Holiness' first trial of strength was against the monster Error; his second will be against a champion called 'Sansfoy'—literally, 'without faith.' "[34] By the third edition, Smith sharpens the allegorical reference. His

footnote now refers to Redcrosse's "second trial against Sansfoy—
'without faith,' atheism."[35] Smith frames an allegorical struggle
fully contained within Christian culture: an intrafaith rather than
an interfaith battle. "For Holiness, even untried, to defeat atheism
('without faith') was comparatively easy."[36] If Sansfoy is an atheist
rather than a Muslim, the challenge to faith is nondenominational
and raises no troublesome questions of competing claims to religious validity. A few of Smith's other notes imply the viewpoint of
a Christian insider. In glossing Redcrosse's armor, for example, he
explains that it "bears the dents of every Christian's fight against
evil."[37]

The *Longman* in 1999 forcefully revives Sansfoy's Muslim status: "Early modern Europeans commonly represented believers in
a non-Christian faith as infidels or nonbelievers. Sansfoy (as this
knight is later named—literally, 'without faith') is therefore not
actually without a faith, but he is a Saracen and not a Christian."[38]
The new anthology chooses not to frame the allegory from a
Christian insider's perspective. Indeed, the *Longman* Renaissance
editors (Constance Jordan and Clare Carroll) implicitly criticize
the parochial worldview that confuses non-Christian faith with
atheism. It is no simple matter to judge whether the *Longman* footnote or Smith's *Norton* footnote gives more accurate, useful interpretive advice. *Longman* is more attentive to historical context and
more sensitive about religious pluralism, but *Norton* presents a
coherent Christian allegory that fits reasonably well with what we
know of Spenser's intentions. (The *Broadview* footnote awkwardly
combines both approaches: Sansfoy is "Saracen, a Muslim, but rep-
resenting Catholicism."[39]) In any case, the seventh edition of *Norton*
revises Smith's treatment of Sansfoy. Editors Stephen Greenblatt
and George M. Logan now call attention to his Muslim identity—
Redcrosse "smites the 'Saracen' (that is, Muslim) Sansfoy (literally,

'without faith')"—but like Smith, they show more interest in a universalized allegorical struggle than a competition between religious creeds. In Spenser's allegory, they suggest, "the enemies are revealed more often than not to be weirdly dissociated aspects of the knights themselves: when he encounters Sansfoy, Redcrosse has just been faithless to his lady Una."[40] If Smith's allegory was about faithful Christians fending off atheism, Greenblatt and Logan tempt readers away from religious faith toward the secular world of sexual fidelity. This is a topic presumably of equal interest to Christians, atheists, and Muslims, and therefore not religiously divisive.

It was not until the seventh edition that *Norton* included Salman Rushdie, a writer who grew up inside Muslim culture. Sean Shesgreen, who looked through years of *Norton* editorial materials, discovered that this addition stirred controversy. "'A weird proposal is Salman Rushdie,' a period editor snapped at a user's proposal to anthologize him."[41] But readers' interests had shifted, postcolonial texts had gained new prominence, Rushdie had won prizes—and besides, *Longman* was putting him in. So Rushdie found himself part of the first *Norton* of the new century. When editors Jon Stallworthy and David Daiches explained the fatwa that had been proclaimed against Rushdie, they treated the substantive religious issue cautiously: "His novel *The Satanic Verses* was judged by senior religious figures in Iran to have blasphemed the Prophet Mohammad, founder of the Muslim faith." Nevertheless, the note clearly sides with liberal, secular outrage over the fatwa. Rushdie "became symbolic of the vulnerability of the intellectual in the face of fundamentalism. . . . He is his own best critic and has defended his book in an essay, *In Good Faith*."[42] Even a year or two before 9/11, Muslim fundamentalism registered as a threat to the West, and *Norton* positions good literature as the best defense against it.

When the eighth edition came out in 2006—during the darkest period of the American war in Iraq—Jon Stallworthy and Jahan Ramazani made a few revisions to the Rushdie headnote that reflect increased sensitivity to Muslim interests. "His novel *The Satanic Verses* provoked riots in India, Pakistan, and South Africa, and was judged by senior religious figures in Iran to have blasphemed the Prophet Muhammad (called by the offensive name 'Mahound' in the novel), founder of the Muslim faith."[43] No longer does responsibility for the fatwa rest solely with hardcore mullahs in Iran, because Muslims around the world had rioted. More strikingly, *Norton* now explains the nature of the blasphemy and to some extent sympathizes with offended Muslims: Rushdie had used "the offensive name 'Mahound.'"

It turns out that the name of the Prophet raises complications for annotators as well as for authors. One minor but resonant controversy has to do with the spelling of the name. Many Muslims prefer "Muhammad" to "Mohammed" as the more respectful transliteration; "Mohammed" reflects some of the older Orientalist terminology (e.g., "Mohammedism" instead of "Islam"). The seventh edition not only uses the less desirable transliteration but spells the Prophet's name two different ways on facing pages: "Mohammad" becomes "Mohammed."[44] The eighth edition conveys greater respect both with the use of "Muhammad" and a keener proofreading eye. As to the offensiveness of "Mahound," Stallworthy and Ramazani's note provides accurate historical background. The name "Mahound" was deployed in derogatory, demonizing contexts by medieval Christians fearful of the spread of Islam. From a literary point of view, however, the matter is not so clear. Rushdie's use of "Mahound" reanimates a slur and offends pious Muslims, but to some extent his novel refashions the derogatory name and alters its connotations. Referring to his character's "demon-tag" of a name, Rushdie's narrator reflects, "To turn insults into strengths, whigs, tories, Blacks all chose to wear with pride the names they were given in scorn; likewise, our mountain-climbing, prophet-motivated solitary is to be the medieval baby-frightener, the Devil's synonym: Mahound."[45] In explaining Rushdie's use of the offensive "Mahound" as the foundation for the blasphemy charge, the 2006 *Norton* pays respect to Islam but, at the same time, may have compromised its literary sophistication.[46]

The ninth edition brings one more twist in the anthology's careful maneuvers with respect to recent conflicts between Islam and the West. If the 2006 *Norton* made adjustments to accommodate Muslim piety and present a more impartial view of cultural history, in 2012 the editors tweak the Rushdie headnote just a bit in the other direction: "The lifting of the fatwa in 1998 allowed Rushdie to reappear in public, but it is seen as irrevocable by some religious groups, and so his life remains under constant threat. Al-Qaeda was among the groups that condemned his being knighted by Queen Elizabeth II in 2007."[47] The new item about Al-Qaeda, especially alongside a reference to Queen Elizabeth and one of her knights, gives the note a sort of throwback Spenserian feel. We still have a "war" going, it seems to remind us, for all our literary sophistication and cultural pluralism.

QUEER SEXUALITY

With Gerard Manley Hopkins, editors face another delicate case in which literary and religious values compete for priority. All versions of the *Norton* headnote suggest that Hopkins's poetic inclinations came into conflict with his religious commitment. To some degree, in other words, the poet was an adversary for the priest. In his headnote to the first edition, which will remain intact through four editions, David Daiches explains the conflict as a matter of secular aesthetic interests intruding on timeless religious values:

> A devoted Jesuit performing faithfully the duties assigned to him by his superiors, Hopkins was also a sensitive poet fascinated by language and rhythm and a passionately keen observer of the color and form and detail of the world of nature. The claims of religion and the duties of his religious profession were paramount, but his aesthetic interests . . . asserted themselves with sometimes painful force, and it was not always easy for him to reconcile his religious vocation with his poetic genius.[48]

Daiches hints that this conflict had visceral effects on Hopkins, whose sensory life was "passionate" enough to assert itself "with sometimes painful force." For Daiches, religious duty wins out, but at some considerable emotional cost. Starting with the fifth edition, *Norton* moves Hopkins from the Moderns back to the Victorians, where George Ford and Carol Christ pay less attention to Hopkins's success as a Jesuit and more to the poetic impulses. Hopkins burned his early Keats-like poems, "for he believed that his vocation must require renouncing such personal satisfactions as the writing of poems."[49] Here the battle between priest and poet seems more strenuous and structural; instead of aesthetic urges that rise up from time to time, Hopkins faces a constant temptation that must be renounced.

All versions of the headnote devote a paragraph to the "terrible sonnets," a handful of poems in which Hopkins expresses most explicitly his anguish. Daiches offers the following explanation: "Hopkins went through a period of deep depression, of a listless sense of failure, and of that deep spiritual emptiness which mystics know as 'the dark night of the soul' and see as one of the necessary stages on the road to spiritual fulfillment."[50] He strings three descriptions together as if they were variations on the same diagnosis, but they carry very different implications. It is not clear from the headnote which is the primary adversary for Hopkins—a biochemical condition, a secular sense of unfulfilled potential, or a mysterious spiritual affliction. In any case, Daiches shapes a happy ending to his discussion of the terrible sonnets. "But Hopkins also enjoyed moods of intense pleasure in the natural world," he writes, "linked with a profound sense of natural beauty as a reflection of divine reality."[51] Ford and Christ will reverse this rhetorical structure to emphasize the secular pain above the religious resolution. They begin with a description of enthusiastic poems but give the climactic position to his anguish: "In Hopkins' early poetry, his singular apprehension of the beauty of individual objects always brings him to an ecstatic illumination of the presence of God. But in his late poems, the so-called 'terrible sonnets,' his distinctive individuality comes to isolate him from the God who made him thus."[52]

God has made Hopkins "singular" and "distinctive." All editions of *Norton* have left the impression that this singularity refers to a heightened aesthetic sensibility and the impulse to write poetry. If the threat to Hopkins's religious stability amounts to poetic imagination, this sort of adversary presents no difficulties for the world of *Norton*. *Norton* was conceived during the glory days of the New Critical paradigm, which treated the writing and reading of poems with sacramental respect. What no *Norton* has ever raised, however, is a more controversial "adversary" for Hopkins: queer sexual impulses. What if his singularity had some connection with homoerotic desire, and his anguish with the need to repress such feelings? Biographers disagree sharply on this question, but it would seem to merit at least some mention. Well-respected authorities have suggested that Hopkins's life and work might be better understood if hints of sexual repression were given serious consideration. Among those who have made this suggestion are biographer Robert Martin and critics Denis Donoghue and Brad Leithauser. In a recent review of a new Hopkins biography, David E. Anderson complains, "One of the curious lacunae in Mariani's book is any serious discussion of Hopkins and sex, especially the contentious issue of whether Hopkins was homosexual. . . . It may well be irresolvable, but one wishes Mariani had taken up the issue."[53] Why has *Norton* remained silent about the debate?

It is not as if the anthology has resisted annotative adaptations that reflect the new prominence of queer studies—quite the contrary, in fact. But Hopkins appears to be a special case. There may be one very practical factor influencing *Norton*'s decision. The ill-fated *Oxford*, never a viable competitor to *Norton* despite celebrity editors, had prominently raised the matter of homosexuality in its headnote to Hopkins. Harold Bloom no doubt irritated many professors with his bold approach to the poet's life. "His more properly poetic anguish is wholly Romantic, like Arnold's," declares Bloom, "for it derives both from a baffled or repressed sexual passion (possibly homosexual, in Hopkins) and from an incurably Romantic sensibility desperately striving not to be Romantic, but to make a return to a lost tradition." As he continues, Bloom makes his sexual suggestion more robust: at Oxford, "Hopkins underwent a crisis, which came in March 1865 and resulted from meeting an enthusiastic, very young, and beautiful religious poet, Digby Dolben, who was to drown in June 1867 at the age of 19. That Hopkins fell in love with Dolben is quite likely, and it is also possible that his subsequent aesthetic revulsion away from the world was, on an unconscious level, a revulsion away from his own desires."[54]

With other writers, Norton steadily updated its information about queer sexuality. Early editions omitted the subject, but later editions included it and gradually adapted annotative rhetoric to suit evolving values. The case of Byron provides a helpful example. As with Hopkins, biographers have disagreed about Byron's "essential" sexual identity and how much importance to attach to his intimate relationships with men. Abrams's original headnote, ample as it was, made no mention of the subject. By the third edition, he inserted two references. Both are meant to be strictly informational, but in both cases the rhetoric implies something inherently destructive about homosexual behavior. "Byron seems to have had one attribute in common with the Byronic hero—a compulsion to try forbidden experience (including, as we now know, homosexual love affairs), joined with a tendency to court his own destruction."[55] The connection between homosexuality and destruction reappears near the end of the headnote, when Abrams describes Byron's death in Greece: "In the dismal, marshy town of Missolonghi he lived a Spartan existence, undertaking to train troops whom he had himself subsidized and exhibiting great practical grasp and power of leadership amid an incredible confusion of factionalism, intrigue, and military ineptitude, and despite an unhappy passion for his Greek page boy, Loukas. Worn out, he succumbed to a series of feverish attacks and died just after he had reached his 36th birthday."[56] Abrams tags Byron's passion for the page boy "unhappy" and implicitly associates it with marshy, feverish decay.

Shesgreen found a comment from one professor who criticized the Byron headnote for its "yoking homosexuality to self-destruction—setting up the homosexual = destroyer equation." According to Shesgreen, Abrams "wrote a personal letter apologizing for his inadvertence and promising remedy in the next edition."[57] The remedy happened in stages. The fifth edition removed mention of the Greek page boy, but left intact the parenthetical reference to "homosexual love affairs" in a context of self-destruction. Both passages disappeared from the seventh edition, which made no mention at all of sex with men. Abrams and Stillinger had learned to be cautious, but removing the subject altogether turned out to be a false step. The eighth edition restores the references but adapts them to reflect new attitudes toward queer sexuality. Editors Stillinger and Deirdre Lynch renormalize this aspect of Byron's life by reference to historical context: young Byron traveled to Greece and Asia Minor, where, "in the classic locale for Greek love, he encountered a culture that accepted sexual relations between older aristocratic men and beautiful boys, and he accumulated materials that, sometimes rather slyly, he incorporated into many of his important poems."[58]

The evolution of notes about Byron's queer sexuality follows a pattern seen in other relevant cases (e.g., Shakespeare, Oscar Wilde, Virginia Woolf). Early on the topic is left out; then it enters, but with subtle, presumably unintended pejorative connotations; finally, connotations are cleaned up to reflect contemporary sexual pluralism. Hopkins stands as a thought-provoking exception to this pattern. The deviation can be explained by a combination of factors, including respect for his Jesuit devotion, murky biographical evidence, and the cautionary example of *Oxford*. The only conceivable hint dropped in *Norton* first appears in the fifth edition, as the editors reflect on Hopkins's Victorian literary affiliations. Whereas early editions had cited only Robert Browning as Hopkins's ally in poetic experimentation, the fifth edition cites a new triad of unconventional Victorians: "Like Algernon Charles Swinburne, Walter Pater, and Henry James as well as Browning, Hopkins displays a new mannerism, characteristic of the latter part of the 19th century, which paradoxically combines an elaborate aestheticism with a more complex representation of consciousness."[59] All three of these new colleagues have well-established connections with queer sexuality. But it is not at all clear that *Norton* means to suggest anything beyond its explicit point about literary style.

Whatever the intentions of the editors, a *Norton* reader can find only this subtlest of clues about the risky question of Hopkins's sexuality. The *Longman*, on the other hand, while declining to make any explicit, Bloom-style reference to queer sexuality, provides a much bolder hint. Editors Heather Henderson and William Sharpe end their headnote with this coy but highly suggestive clue: "And yet, Hopkins did recognize that his mingling of sensuality and spirituality allied him with another great proto-Modernist: 'I always knew in my heart Walt Whitman's mind to be more like my own than any other man's living,' he told Bridges. 'As he is a great scoundrel this is not a pleasant confession.'"[60] *Longman's* comparison carries more weight than *Norton's* invocation of Swinburne, Pater, and James: not only because the editors position it as a climax, but because it is Hopkins himself who "confesses" this affiliation. *Longman* appears to have deployed an annotative trope—something we might call "conspicuous implication"—that allows the editors to say something provocative about Hopkins without actually saying it. The note might thereby satisfy both those who welcome this "information" about Hopkins and those who might find it misleading or offensive.

In a contemporary world increasingly sensitized to the consequences of religious divisions and surrounding cultural differences, anthologies competing for survival might find such annotative camouflage a useful adaptive strategy. *Longman's* remark about Hopkins looks innocuous enough to an eye trained to process information about intraliterary genealogies: the note's explicit message, after all, records only a literary affiliation between Hopkins and Whitman ("proto-Modernism"). Indeed, the only insider's perspective that has ever been perfectly safe for an anthology editor is that of a literary enthusiast. In the current marketplace for anthologies, however, with both *Longman* and *Norton* pinning their advertising on broadened coverage of cultural topics—all curated in conformity with the newest secular values—it would be as risky to retreat inside a literary bubble as to resume the old-fashioned deference to Christian interests.

Chapter 5

The Curious Case of Pope Francis

Francis has brought to his papacy an intriguing entanglement of the old and the new. He has inspired many Catholics—and unsettled some—with ideas and attitudes that seem surprisingly in tune with secular interests. His notable gestures of this sort include matters of Church doctrine, social policy, and science. Francis has suggested, among other things, that even atheists can get to heaven; that homosexuals are to be welcomed as God's beloved; that women who have had abortions or divorces should be granted easier re-entry to sacramental communion; that corporate greed and many elements of our global economic structure are to be condemned as anti-Christian; that misusing the earth's resources amounts to a sin; and that fighting global warming is a moral obligation.

It is Pope Francis's secular-friendly modernity that has mainly captured the attention of the world. Both Catholics and non-Catholics have been struck by his iconoclastic approaches to various elements of church tradition. But there is another side to this man, not a modern iconoclast but something very nearly its opposite. Francis has shown a real passion for archaic devotional practices that contemporary Catholics consider borderline superstitious, notably the veneration of relics and sacred icons; and he also has made it clear that he believes in the literal presence of Satan and his demons. Some of his actions and comments seem more properly medieval than modern. How can we understand what appear to be two contrary identities within Pope Francis, one so new and the other so old?

If we look to the biographies of Francis, one moment particularly stands out for its relevance to this question. It hints at an entanglement of modern and archaic perspectives in the future Pope, even when he was a young man. Jorge Bergoglio was busy training to be an industrial chemist at Escuela Industrial No. 12 in Buenos Aires. As he advanced in his studies, something old suddenly altered his life plan. He had started working in the Hickethier-Bachmann chemical laboratory, under the direction of someone he very much admired, Esther Ballestrino de Careaga. She taught him scientific rigor and also happened to be an atheist, with political interests in the sufferings of her native Paraguay. One day during this period of working at the lab, Bergoglio felt an inexplicable impulse to enter a nearby church. He went into a confessional, talked with the local priest, and suddenly the young man knew he had a compelling vocation to become a priest. He later described the experience as "like being thrown from a horse."[1] The young chemist, in other words, likened himself to St. Paul on the road to Damascus, miraculously inspired (and unhorsed) by God's calling. But he continued to work in his lab alongside the admirable atheist. For young Bergoglio, the miracle of his calling complicated, but did not displace, his secular identity.

ST. JANUARIUS'S BLOOD AND THE SHROUD OF TURIN

Bergoglio's actions since he became pope offer other useful evidence for anyone trying to sort out the old and the new in Francis.

Two visits give indications of his interest in old-fashioned devotional objects. He traveled to Naples in March of 2015 for various public and private events. One stop took him to the city's cathedral, where he performed a ceremony involving the famous old relic of St. Januarius (Gennaro). Januarius, an early martyr during the persecutions of the emperor Diocletian, supposedly had both his head and samples of his blood preserved after his decapitation. The head is enshrined in an ornate bust; the blood sits in a tightly sealed vial inside a silver reliquary. Beginning in the fourteenth century, the blood of Januarius would on occasion mysteriously liquefy when the bishop of Naples picked it up and moved it near the bust containing the head. Ordinarily the blood remains congealed and opaque in its vial. When the supposed miracles occur, however, the blood bubbles, fills more of the interior space, and turns a reddish color. The Naples bishops perform the ceremony three times a year. Sometimes the miracle occurs; sometimes it does not. Many locals believe that when the saint signifies his blessing through the tangible change of his blood, it will bring them prosperity (including the taming of Mount Vesuvius). They expect trouble when the miracle does not take place.

The miracle did *not* take place when Francis's two predecessors made their visits and held the blood. John Paul II saw no bubbling in 1979, nor did Benedict in 2007 (although, rather sadly, he waited about an hour for something to happen). But when Francis took up the vial and kissed it at the cathedral altar, the attending bishop saw the supposedly miraculous transformation begin on cue. "When Crescenzio Sepe, the Cardinal of the Diocese, initially gave the relic to the Pope, the blood was still solid on one side of the vial; however when Pope Francis returned the reliquary, the cardinal looked at the relic and then announced, 'It seems that St. Januarius loves the Pope, because the blood is already half liquefied.'"[2]

Francis's response to the fresh miracle was surprising, and a little hard to read. After receiving the news, he told the congregation, "The bishop just announced that the blood half-liquefied. We can see the saint only half loves us. If only half of it liquefied that means we still have work to do; we have to do better. We must all spread the Word, so that he loves us more!"[3] Both those attracted to Francis the New and those who prefer Francis the Old might reasonably interpret his response as support for their position. On the side of the Old, he did acknowledge the miracle as something real; he encouraged the faithful to take it seriously as a sign of divine favor or disfavor. And of course he kissed and venerated it with genuine devotion. Those who appreciate Francis the New, however, could point to the tone of his remark as evidence for his contemporary sophistication. It seems a little odd that he would say something ironic, almost snarky, after seeing what he really believed was a miracle take place in his own hands. With his reply, the emphasis shifts from God's miracle to man's wit. Supporters of Francis the New will not find it difficult to discount his apparent reliance on ancient superstition, as embarrassing as it might seem on the surface. They will likely conclude that he was merely humoring the good people of Naples.

It is very hard to say whether the scientist in Francis secretly laughs at the miracle of St. Januarius's blood. Before he started on his path to ordination, he trained as an analytical chemist and worked in a lab evaluating the nutritional content of various foods. At least part of his mind must look at the substance in the vial and see an ordinary physical change, explainable by natural causes— explainable, that is, if the Church would allow the reliquary to be opened and subjected to chemical analysis. Although no such permission has been granted, scientists from the eighteenth century on have expressed skepticism about the supposed miracle. They have proposed a few scientific explanations to debunk the miracle.

The blood may liquefy because it heats up slightly (a person handling the relic makes it a little warmer, and the space crowded with onlookers may contribute to this effect); or it might happen because the vial is moved and shaken, after months of sitting still. Both of these theories would make better sense if another debunking theory could be verified: skeptics have suggested that the substance inside the reliquary might not be blood at all, or at best might contain only traces of blood. Chemists have tested certain oils and waxes with very low boiling points and found that they could approximate the "miraculous" events inside the vial. This theory of pseudoblood gains more credibility because it turns out that the Naples region has more or less specialized in such relics. "Probably the most serious difficulty against the miraculous character of the phenomenon," acknowledges the *Catholic Encyclopedia*, "is derived from the circumstances that the same liquefaction takes place in the case of other relics, nearly all preserved in the neighborhood of Naples, or of Neapolitan origin."[4]

The *Catholic Encyclopedia* does not take a stand on St. Januarius's blood. It neither affirms nor refutes its miraculous character. The modern Catholic Church for the most part welcomes the work of science: the Church has apologized for its mistreatment of Galileo, embraced the Big Bang and evolution, and in general appreciated scientific discoveries for the light they shed on God's creation. It is also true that their essential articles of faith include several beliefs that science cannot explain, that must remain in the province of the supernatural and miraculous. Some obvious examples include the virgin birth, the resurrection, sacramental transubstantiation, and the miraculous healings attributed to saints (and taken as proof for their canonization). Many other possibly supernatural events and related objects belong to the category of "popular devotion," which means that the Church does not require the faithful to accept their authenticity as a matter of sacred truth. They might be authentic, and they might not. The case of the liquefaction of Januarius's blood is a good example: Catholics are free to believe it or not believe it as they see fit. To which camp does Pope Francis belong? The analytical chemist and the medieval devotee seem to be making equally strong claims. I would suggest that the best approach is not to make this an either-or proposition. The chemist and the devotee present an entanglement, not a dichotomy.

A few months later, Francis visited another object of popular devotion, the Shroud of Turin, and again gave mixed signals of an old and new approach. In June of 2015, he went to the cathedral in Turin to venerate the famous cloth, which many Catholics believe wrapped the dead body of Jesus after it was removed from the cross. "Francis sat for several minutes before the Shroud, which is contained in a protective glass case. He lowered his head at times in apparent reflection and occasionally gazed up at the 4.3 meter cloth. Then he took a few steps, placed his hand on the case, and walked away without comment."[5]

The Shroud of Turin is probably the best known among objects that Catholics popularly venerate. As in the case of St. Januarius's blood, the Church has not officially confirmed or debunked its authenticity. It first became known to the Christian world in the fourteenth century, but it was not until 1898 that the supposed burial cloth became a sensation. An Italian photographer named Secondo Pia photographed the image on the shroud, which looks like "the vague sepia blur of a human body. But when Pia examined the reverse negative of his photographic plate in the darkroom, he discovered the detailed likeness of a bearded man with visible wounds on his body."[6]

The Vatican in this case gave scientists good access to the object for testing. The first comprehensive tests were carried out by an American-led enterprise called the Shroud of Turin Research Project (STURP), which included thirty-three university scientists from a number of disciplines. In 1981, STURP reported results that encouraged believers: "The Shroud image is that of a real human form of a scourged, crucified man. It is not the product of an artist. The blood stains are composed of hemoglobin and also gave a positive test for serum albumin." They declined to say more, however, about who that man might have been and when and how the image was produced. The Shroud "remains now, as it has in the past, a mystery."[7]

Other scientists pursued the problem of dating the cloth. In 1988, scientists from three separate teams (Oxford, University of Arizona, and the Swiss Federal Institute of Technology) reported the results of their carbon dating: the fabric dates to sometime between 1260 and 1390. Obviously, this was discouraging news for those hoping that the Shroud was an authentic relic rather than a medieval forgery. In subsequent years, other scientists have disputed the findings of the carbon daters. A study in 2010 by Marco Riani of the University of Parma and Anthony Atkinson of the London School of Economics suggested that uneven sampling of the cloth led the carbon daters astray: "The dating which comes from a piece at the top edge is very different from the date which comes from a piece taken from the bottom edge."[8] But the three teams stand by their work, and the case for medieval origin remains quite plausible. The most recent scientific study of the Shroud involved DNA testing. Lead investigator Gianni Barcaccia of the University of Padua reported some results that might encourage enthusiasts—"the strongest genetic signals seemed to come from areas in and around the Middle East and the Caucasus"—but overall he could offer no confirmation of where or when it was produced. "Individuals from different ethnic groups and geographical locations came into contact with the Shroud," he concluded, "but we cannot say anything more on its origin."[9]

Pope Francis, with his background in practical science, no doubt kept up with these results. When the Shroud was made available for a special televised display in 2013, Francis referred to it as "an icon of a man scourged and crucified."[10] He did not cite a source for his remark, but the phrasing comes directly from the 1981 STURP report. Vatican observers noted his cautious use of the word "icon" rather than "relic." John Paul II had called the Shroud a relic when he visited back in 1980. If Francis the Old throws himself into venerating a crucified man, Francis the New holds himself back from identifying the image on the Shroud with the actual body of Jesus.

To return to Francis's visit in 2015, the Pope initially kept silent following his solemn veneration of the cloth in the case. After he celebrated mass in the public square, though, he offered his reflections occasioned by his time with the Shroud. He spoke of Jesus's love for humanity: "The icon of this love is the Shroud, that, even now, has attracted so many people here to Turin. The Shroud draws [people] to the tormented face and body of Jesus and, at the same time, directs [people] toward the face of every suffering and unjustly persecuted person."[11] Both Francis the Old and Francis the New leave their imprints here. Old Francis comes tantalizingly close to confirming its status as a relic when he refers to "the tormented face and body of Jesus." But he stops short of turning an icon into a relic. In fact, he swerves away from this particular object of devotion to focus on the suffering of contemporary humans. This is Francis in his modern mode: what matters is not a maybe-real relic but the undeniably real social and economic conditions that oppress so many in the world. During the Pope's two-day visit to Turin, an industrial city, he repeatedly criticized injustice and a corporate economy indifferent to workers. The Shroud of Turin, already less a relic than an icon, for the moment becomes less an icon than a political signifier.

Catholics who appreciate the modern Pope Francis may find his entanglement with old devotions somewhat embarrassing. But the entanglement is hard to ignore. Taylor Marshall, a liberal Catholic blogger, worries that "sophisticated non-Catholics" will react badly to Francis's attention to suspect relics like St. Januarius's blood and the Shroud of Turin, and think to themselves: "This is shanty town syncretism at best, or ignorant magic at its worst."[12] Many modern Catholics become uncomfortable when they encounter what they consider superstitious devotions that border on idolatry. In their official statement on the subject of "Popular Devotional Practices," American bishops warned that "popular religiosity . . . is often subject to penetration by many distortions of religion and even superstitions."[13] The *Catholic Encyclopedia* refers to the veneration of relics as, "to some extent, a primitive instinct." Many of the objects "duly exhibited for veneration in the great sanctuaries of Christendom or even at Rome itself must now be pronounced to be either certainly spurious or open to grave suspicion."[14] As far back as the Council of Trent in the mid-sixteenth century, Church leaders worried about superstition displacing authentic belief; they decreed that "no new miracles are to be acknowledged or new relics recognized" unless a bishop scrupulously confirms them. The clear trend in Catholicism has been to de-emphasize relics and the miracles associated with them. "There is nothing in the Catholic teaching to justify the statement," says the *Catholic Encyclopedia*, "that the Church encourages belief in a magical virtue, or physical curative efficacy residing in the relic itself."[15]

Pope Francis's order, the Society of Jesus, has a reputation as the most up-to-date and intellectually sophisticated Catholic elite. When a youngish Jorge Bergoglio became head of the Jesuits in

Argentina, his attachment to archaic devotions caused friction. Biographer Paul Vallely describes how Bergoglio walked with peasants as they venerated an icon of the Virgin—an icon associated with a local miracle that caused the image to be deposited in that town. "Many intellectuals discount such legends as the residue of a superstitious peasant religion. Bergoglio never has, and that faultline was one of the subjects of the entrenched disputes he was to have in later years within the Jesuit order."[16] (Jesuit discontent with Bergoglio eventually boiled over, and he was removed from his post and sent into exile.) Vallely adds that Bergoglio "brought the religious style of popular piety" to the seminary where young Jesuits studied: "Seminarians were encouraged to go into the chapel at night and touch or kiss statues and images. . . . Cerebral old-school eyebrows were raised."[17]

POPULAR PIETY, POLITICS, AND PLACEBO

Francis's enthusiasm for popular piety—or more pejoratively, "superstitious peasant religion"—poses a problem for intellectually sophisticated Catholics as well as his many secular admirers. Might there be a way to reconcile the Francis they admire with these strains of neomedieval devotion that raise secular eyebrows? Two theories might be proposed to make the Old Francis compatible with the New Francis. From a political perspective, his embrace of popular piety could be viewed as consistent with his radical critique of contemporary socioeconomic conditions and the infrastructure that generates inequality. From a more scientific perspective, the pope may have good reason to assume that *belief* in relics and miracles provides authentic therapeutic and spiritual value—regardless of the authenticity of the relics themselves.

Bergoglio in his younger years as a Jesuit leader disdained Liberation Theology. He had grown up in the polarizing atmosphere of the Cold War; for him, Liberation Theology amounted to a dangerous alliance with communist ideology and its atheistic fundamentals. Vallely quotes a Jesuit from that time: "Liberation Theology was actually forbidden. . . . It was seen by him as very suspicious if you were interested in that."[18] But the older Bergoglio who became Pope Francis had completely changed his mind on this subject. The collapse of the Soviet Union had dramatically altered the geopolitical scene. With the threat of Soviet atheism no longer a factor, Bergoglio turned his attention to the deleterious effects of global capitalism. As Vallely puts it, "[T]he authoritarian conservative" who annoyed so many liberal Jesuits had now "transformed from the scourge of Liberation Theology to a Pope for the poor."[19]

The pope's transformation was not a matter of him suddenly discovering a concern for the impoverished and marginalized. The younger Bergoglio certainly had such concerns, despite his distaste for communist approaches to solving socioeconomic problems. He wanted the Church to do its best to alleviate the ill effects of poverty in Argentina's underclasses. His later embrace of more radical approaches meant he gave more attention to challenging the status quo (as opposed to merely treating the symptoms of a flawed system), but his core concern for the poor did not change. One key feature of Bergoglio's pastoral care has always been to recognize the importance of popular piety. As biographer Austin Ivereigh explains, only in the big cities of Argentina had the Church established a foundation of sustaining institutions—especially parishes and schools, with accompanying nuns and priests. In the country's interior, "the dioceses remained vast, poor and remote," so that "the rural poor continued . . . to have little contact with the Church."[20] Given the isolation of these communities, practices of popular devotion competed with, even displaced, the regular Church worship. "Popular religion—which Bergoglio would always respect as an evangelical culture," writes Ivereigh, "has its origin here: country people ignorant of doctrine but with deep faith who, in the absence of clergy and churches, looked to devotions more than sacraments."[21]

The Bergoglio who alarmed liberal Jesuits chose not to correct or curtail but to embrace these nonsacramental devotions. When he was Archbishop of Buenos Aires, he encouraged (and funded) a poor community with Paraguayan roots to retrieve an icon of the Virgin that they credited with miraculous powers. The local priest took up the icon and marched it through the squalor of their shanty town. As Vallely narrates, "Cheering crowds gathered on such a scale that Archbishop Bergoglio held a special Mass for people of the slum—but invited them into the cathedral to celebrate it." Bergoglio afterwards joined the people as they returned home with their icon held high: "Bergoglio, wearing a poncho and carrying his rosary beads, slipped surreptitiously in among the procession."[22]

It seems reasonable to suggest that Pope Francis's enthusiasm for archaic devotions is consistent with his modern political liberalism. The bishop in a poncho marching behind a miraculous icon has found a way to shed privilege and perform acts of progressive inclusion. The old and new, in this context, seem to join forces rather than split apart. However, the rationale behind this reconciliation of old and new is subject to challenge. Modern critics of the archaic Francis may still find reason to raise their eyebrows at his embrace of dubious relics and icons. Liberal Jesuits, according to Vallely, saw his "obsession with culture and pious popular practices as an unhelpful diversion. Popular piety could so turn poor people's attention to the next world that they succumbed to a fatalist resignation instead of pressing for improvements in the economic and social structures."[23]

THE CURIOUS CASE OF POPE FRANCIS

Popular piety, in other words, might be no more than Marx's old opium dished out to the oppressed to keep them tame. As much as Francis the New has aggressively challenged the settled geopolitical order, Francis the Old might plausibly be blamed for distracting his flock from their real needs. The entanglement of old and new does not simply resolve in favor of the new.

A second theory for understanding this entanglement has to do with science rather than politics. We might frame his attachment to archaic devotions as a scientific question: does this sort of thing actually work? If science can prove the benefits of certain devotional practices, then Pope Francis may have a new way of justifying his attachment to the old modes of devotion.

Quite a number of studies have been published that test the efficacy of religious activities in promoting health. Many of these studies have focused on "Intercessory Prayer" (IP)—in other words, prayers offered up on behalf of another person in ill health or undergoing surgery. These kinds of study are notoriously difficult to design (especially because many of the relevant variables are hard to quantify), and the results prove difficult to interpret. Several authors of such studies claim that IP confers significant therapeutic benefits. The earliest and most enthusiastic papers date from the 1980s and 1990s. After scientists raised methodological concerns about these studies, researchers became more cautious in their conclusions, even as their data suggested the benefits of prayer. A 2012 review article concludes, "The results of prayer on specific disease states appear inconsistent with cardiovascular disease but stronger in other disease states."[24] Other scientists have shown more skepticism. The highly regarded Cochrane Database of Systematic Reviews delivered an assessment of "Intercessory Prayer for the Alleviation of Ill Health" in 2008, and their conclusions deflated champions of IP. "These findings are equivocal and, although some of the results of individual studies suggest a positive effect of IP, the majority do not and the evidence does not support a recommendation either in favor or against the use of IP."[25] The Cochrane review team showed little sympathy for what they considered an ill-advised marriage of religious and scientific paradigms; they even recommended that no further resources be devoted to such studies.

The studies have continued, however, and many scientists find the question of IP's value complex and nuanced. In her 2012 book *Testing Prayer: Science and Healing,* Candy Gunther Brown gives respectful attention to both the critics and the advocates of IP. Brown concludes that *"perceived* divine healing experiences have the potential to exert lasting effects—not only on the person claiming healing but also on family members and friends."[26] The rituals of IP affect physical and mental well-being; those who experience healing from IP "credit divine love and power for their recoveries, and they consequently feel motivated to express greater love for God and other people."[27] Scientists of faith would also assume that God caused the healing (although they could not of course prove or report this in a scientific paper). Secular scientists who find evidence that IP heals must look elsewhere for a causal explanation.

The most plausible causal explanation for IP's therapeutic benefits comes from the emerging science of placebos. In the passage quoted above, Brown carefully refers to *"perceived* divine healing experiences," rendering moot the validity of theistic claims about God's real intervention. One study tracked two groups of patients: those who received IP, and those who expected to receive IP but did not. The authors found that "the effects of IP and positive visualization cannot be distinguished from the effect of expectancy."[28] Patients who believed that people were praying for them did just as well as those actually prayed for. The implication seems clear: it is not the prayers themselves that do the good work; it is the patient's placebo-receptive mind.

A placebo effect can be defined as a favorable response to some sort of intervention that has no direct physiological effect. Doctors have acknowledged for a long time that placebos work for some percentage of their patients, but only in recent years have studies shown that placebos trigger physical changes in the brain. As a Harvard Medical School report summarizes, "Research is showing that the placebo effect often seems to be associated with objective changes in brain chemistry. A number of studies have shown, for example, that the brain releases natural pain-relieving substances called endorphins when people enrolled in pain studies are given placebos."[29] Harvard scientist Ted Kaptchuk has led the way in placebo studies. In some of his recent work, Kaptchuk has tested the effectiveness of what he calls "the ritual of medicine." One group of patients was simply given a placebo, without any persona attention; but for another group, doctors spent twenty minutes with each patient—conversing, touching, and spending at least twenty seconds "lost in thoughtful silence."[30] Those who received their placebos with full ritual ended up having the greatest relief of symptoms. As researcher Fabrizio Benedetti puts it, "What we 'placebo neuroscientists' have learned is that therapeutic rituals move a lot of molecules in the patient's brain."[31]

In placebo experiments, an object with no objective therapeutic value—placebos, after all, cannot cure infections or shrink cancerous tumors—combines with ritual to make patients feel significantly better. When Pope Francis conducts his rituals with objects of dubious authenticity, the beneficial effects on people in Naples or Turin or Buenos Aires might be substantial. If we posit for the sake of argument that all relics or miraculous icons have no real supernatural powers, it is nonetheless important to recognize a placebo effect: participating in a healing ceremony with a sacred object may very well enhance someone's physical, psychological, and spiritual well-being. Francis may have good scientific reasons to take advantage of the placebo value of old relics. But it is impossible to say with any confidence that this pope does *not* believe in the miraculous powers of such relics. His old and new interests remain too entangled to separate one or the other as the primary mode of explanation.

THE FRANCIS EFFECT: OLD DEMONS IN THE NEW CHURCH

In the matter of Pope Francis's other throwback interest—his belief in Satan as a literal presence in the world, an active agent of evil— the evidence does not seem ambiguous. Here the medieval Francis does not easily yield to modern reinterpretation. Pope Francis has harped on Satan and demonic influence from the beginning of his papacy. His Vatican put out an urgent call for more exorcists to meet the increasing demand for their services.

To frame this subject, it might be helpful to recall something C. S. Lewis said in *The Screwtape Letters*. Screwtape was the name Lewis gave to a veteran demon who wrote letters of advice to his unproven nephew Wormwood. In the introduction to his demonic epistolary fiction, Lewis remarked, "There are two equal and opposite errors, into which our race can fall about the devils. One is to disbelieve in their existence. The other is to believe, and feel an excessive and unhealthy interest in them. They themselves are equally pleased and hail a materialist and a magician with the same delight."[32] The contemporary Catholic Church shows symptoms of both errors described by Lewis. Many modern Catholics do not believe that Satan is an actual being who causes trouble in the world. For them, references to Satan should be understood as metaphorical representations of evil; instances of demonic possession are properly explained as mental illness. At the other extreme, some contemporary Catholics believe in the devil so passionately that their interest might be considered "excessive and unhealthy," as Lewis put it. A good candidate for this second error would be the Roman exorcist Gabriele Amorth, who claims to have performed thirty thousand exorcisms, and warns people against doing yoga and reading *Harry Potter*. If Pope Francis risks affiliation with either group, it would be the second one. Most of Francis's liberal admirers both within and outside the Church would fall into the first group, those who consider Satan merely a metaphor.

The modern skeptical position gained traction in the 1960s, when the revolutionary Second Vatican Council questioned many assumptions of the traditional Church. One of the traditional ideas that lost support was Satan as a literal agent in the world. Church doctrine did not officially change: the catechism then as now explains that Satan's influence "may cause grave injuries—of a spiritual nature, and indirectly, even of a physical nature—to each man and to society." But according to Notre Dame historian R. Scott Appleby, "the influence of the Second Vatican Council in the early 1960s and the broader ecumenical movement, together with a greater interest by church authorities in the behavioral sciences, pushed aside much discussion of hell and the Devil."[33] A study of Catholic sermons in the 1980s showed that Satan and demonic influence "had diminished markedly" as a topic for parish priests.[34] The trend to diminish or eliminate Satan became so evident that a conservative Catholic think tank felt compelled to argue against it. The Congregation for the Doctrine of the Faith published a document to counteract what they called "postmodern skepticism about the existence of Satan and other evil spirits."[35]

Skepticism about Satan came in part from theological argument—the scriptural foundations for belief in Satan are minimal, and open to a variety of interpretations. But the greater challenge came from the increasing sophistication of psychiatric science. Psychiatrists could retrospectively diagnose biblical victims of demonic possession: they were actually suffering an epileptic seizure, or a schizophrenic breakdown, or some other natural brain disorder. The *Diagnostic and Statistical Manual of Mental Disorders* in its current iteration (*DSM-5*) uses the category of "Dissociative Identity Disorder" to address episodes of delusion involving demonic influence.[36] Dissociative Identity Disorder refers to cases when a patient's sense of self is not stably integrated; often he or she shows signs of more than one identity competing for control. As the Church absorbed modern psychiatric models, most of what used to be classified as demonic influence was now explainable, and treatable, as mental illness. Vatican guidelines in the later decades of the twentieth century advised that most episodes of demonic possession were nothing of the sort. For almost all symptoms of supposed possession, priests were to rely on psychiatrists rather than exorcists.

Pope Francis has set himself in stark opposition to modern (or as some prefer, postmodern) skepticism about Satan. It might be unfair to accuse him of C. S. Lewis's second error—an "excessive and unhealthy interest" in devils—but he has shown such a vivid interest in Satan that one priest wrote an article for CNN with the title, "Why Is Pope Francis So Obsessed with the Devil?" The author of that article, Reverend Thomas Rosica, begins by noting how many of Francis's tweets and sermons include references to "the Devil, Satan, the Accuser, the Evil One, the Father of Lies, the Ancient Serpent, the Tempter, the Seducer, the Great Dragon, the Enemy, and just plain 'demon.'"[37] Another article summarizes the abrupt change from previous popes. "Unlike his recent predecessors, who seemingly preferred to talk about anything but the Devil, Pope Francis is consistently mentioning he who, in modern Catholicism, must not be named."[38] Vatican insiders refer to "The Francis Effect": since he became pope, more and more Catholics have reported experiences of demonic possession. He has also brought the Devil into analysis of world affairs. Francis told an audience in Mexico that demonic influence was responsible for the country's drug wars; he has also implicated Satan in the crises of the Middle East.

When Pope Francis said Mass in public one day in 2013, he gave a sermon based on the Gospel reading. The passage, from Luke, described a moment when Jesus cast out demons. Francis began his sermon by acknowledging the modern trend to naturalize demonic possession: "There are some priests who, when they read this Gospel passage, say: 'But Jesus healed a person with a mental illness.'" Then he briefly makes a concession to modern thinking: "It is true that at that time, they could confuse epilepsy with demonic possession." But he answers back, "It is also true that there was the Devil! And we do not have the right to simplify the matter as if to say: 'all of these people were not possessed; they were mentally ill.' No!" Francis went on to describe what an encounter with Satan would feel like. "St. Peter would say, it is like a fierce lion that circles us. It is like that." He closes by anticipating objections to Francis the Old: "'But, Father, you are a little ancient. You are frightening us with these things.' No, not me! It is the Gospel!"[39]

In the first year of his papacy, Francis performed what some people took to be an impromptu exorcism. A young Mexican man in a wheelchair had come to Rome to receive the pope's blessing. The man believed that he suffered from demonic possession. When Francis came to his wheelchair, he placed his hands on the man's head and started praying intensely for about ten seconds. The man's head then dropped down. *La Repubblica* consulted with an exorcism expert, who said he thought "it was a prayer of liberation from evil, or even a real exorcism."[40] The Vatican insisted that this was not the case. Pope Francis had performed no exorcism; he had blessed the man with a prayer and a laying on of hands. Later, though, Juan Rivas, the Mexican priest who had accompanied the man in the wheelchair to Rome, told a different story. "The Pope then laid his hands on his head," said Rivas, "and at that moment a terrible sound was heard, like the roar of a lion. All those who were there heard it perfectly well. The pope for sure heard it, but he continued with his prayer, as if he had faced similar situations before."[41]

It is hard to evaluate the reliability of Rivas's account. No one (to my knowledge) has come forward to support his claim of the roaring sound. But his portrait of Francis as exorcist gains a little credibility because the pope later described Satan as "a fierce lion that circles us." As much as the Vatican tries to downplay the medieval drama of literal demons and exorcisms, Francis keeps these older elements alive in his "obsession" with the devil. The pope himself recognizes the awkwardness of his ancient ideas in a modern setting. "But Father, you are a little ancient," he imagined people saying of his "frightening" talk of the devil. Once he mentioned to reporters that visitors "gently chide him, 'But Father, how old-fashioned you are to speak about the Devil in the twenty-first century!' " To which Francis replied, "Look out, because the Devil is present."[42]

How, then, can we account for Pope Francis's throwback fascination with Satan and his demonic legions? Although the medieval content of his message is undeniable, there are two ways of interpreting his obsession with devils that can help us understand it as an entanglement of old and new. One is pragmatic: Francis invokes demons in order to bolster his efforts to fix Church corruption. The second interpretation is more theoretical. One critic has proposed that something is missing from our contemporary paradigms for understanding evil; perhaps, he argues, the ancient idea of Satan offered a way of talking about behavior that science by itself cannot explain.

When Francis became pope, he immediately focused on eliminating corruption within the Vatican. His predecessor Pope Benedict had been ineffectual in his governance of Church bureaucracy. Francis made it clear that he wanted to reform the structure and powers of the Roman Curia, the centralized group that administers Church affairs. Francis would prefer a more decentralized approach to Church governance, which would diminish the powers of the inner circle. He also took steps to reform the way the Vatican handles its finances; under the new pope's scrutiny, many questionable banking practices came to light. And Francis condemned clerical sexual abuse more vigorously than any previous pope. Francis may feel he has some leverage, since polls show he is the most popular pope ever: he has a favorable rating of 85 percent among Catholics, 53 percent among Protestants, and a remarkable 51 percent among atheists. Still, internal Vatican opposition to Francis has been strong. As a BBC reporter summarizes, "Within the Curia, the pope has polarized opinion. . . . Not all of Pope Francis' reforms are proving so popular and some are encountering stiff internal resistance. Any honeymoon period within the Curia for this pope is long since over."[43]

Given the strength of opposition to his reforms, one of Pope Francis's most powerful weapons has been his invocation of demonic influence. Although he never explicitly accused any Vatican official of Satanic connections, he has made a number of comments that subtly associate demons with Church insiders. Once he said in a sermon, "The Devil is intelligent, he knows more theology than all the theologians together."[44] On Palm Sunday in 2013 he preached that although Jesus is nearby when a Christian faces trouble, "so is the enemy—the Devil," who "comes often disguised as an angel and slyly speaks his word to us."[45] In a book he wrote before becoming pope, Bergoglio insisted that Satan is real, and said that "his fruits are always destruction: division, hate, and slander."[46] This version of the Devil suggests the sort of social and political infighting that afflicts most institutions—certainly including the Church—and that Bergoglio had experienced so bitterly with the Jesuits. If Francis sets out the possibility of devils posing as angels, he calls into question the virtue of his Vatican opponents and justifies his bold positions. Viewed from this perspective, the entanglement of Old Francis with New Francis serves a single, significant goal: cleaning up a corrupt Catholic Church.

There is anther way of understanding in modern terms Pope Francis's emphasis on Satan—this one more philosophical than political. In his 1995 book *The Death of Satan*, Andrew Delbanco argues that our "progression" beyond belief in Satan has left a void. "Faced with serial killers, maniacal despots, and ruthless genocide," he writes, "we first look for psychological, sociological, or even genetic explanations."[47] But these modern modes of analysis do not provide satisfactory explanations, according to Delbanco; and as a result, "[w]e have no language for connecting our inner lives with the horrors that pass before our eyes. . . . We feel something that our culture no longer gives us the vocabulary to express."[48] Delbanco does not argue for a return to belief in a literal Satan; he is too modern and secular for that. But his book offers a helpful way of understanding Francis's revival of Satan. If our scientific resources cannot deliver adequate explanations for horrendous evil, we need something else to serve. Francis finds the answers he needs in the agency of Satan and his demons.

In cases of supposed demonic possession, the modern answers come from the science of psychiatry. The psychiatrist is the secular counterpart of the exorcist. The modern Catholic Church has prescribed a psychiatrist instead of an exorcist in all but a tiny percentage of apparent demonic possessions, but Pope Francis called for more emphasis on exorcism—and required all dioceses to have a qualified exorcist on staff. Although psychiatry and exorcism may seem irreconcilably different in their assumptions and methods, at least one psychiatrist has reflected on similarities between the two. "Exorcism can be said to be the prototypical form of psychotherapy," wrote Stephen A. Diamond. "Like exorcists, psychotherapists speak in the name of a 'higher being,' be it medical science or some psychological, metaphysical, or spiritual belief system." Both exorcists and psychiatrists "join with the patient in a sacred therapeutic alliance against the wicked and debilitating forces bedeviling them." Diamond blurs the distinction between demonic possession and mental illness. The Catholic Church works hard "to distinguish between so-called *genuine possession* and *pseudo-possession*. But can such a distinction truly be drawn? And, if so, on what grounds?"[49]

Diamond's question is rhetorical, and he means to subvert simple distinctions between modern psychiatric symptoms and the influence of ancient demons. His perspective certainly sheds some light on the entanglement of Old and New Francis. But what if we made the problem a little harder by taking Diamond's question literally: how can a priest (or psychiatrist) know for sure when a person is possessed by a demon? The Church recognizes a list of common symptoms of possession: superhuman strength, speaking in languages not previously known, knowledge of remote events, violent aversion to Christian symbols, even levitation. On the surface, it would seem unlikely that any entanglement of ancient and modern can be sustained in this matter. Believers will see enough to recognize possession, but rational secularists will surely debunk any supernatural content.

It turns out, however, that the chasm between believers and scientists is not unbridgeable. Respected academic psychiatrist Richard

Gallagher, with degrees from Yale and Columbia, writes that he has seen a few cases of genuine possession, unexplainable by any other reasoning. He has been called in as consultant on many cases, and most of the time he can diagnose the patient in the usual psychiatric way. But to his surprise, he occasionally sees someone suddenly speak fluently in foreign languages, tell him something about his private family history, or exhibit unusual strength. (He admits that he has never seen levitation, but says a few colleagues have.) Gallagher writes, "Is it possible to be a sophisticated psychiatrist and believe that evil spirits are, however seldom, assailing humans? Most of my scientific colleagues and friends say no. . . . But careful observation of the evidence presented to me in my career has led me to believe that certain extremely uncommon cases can be explained no other way."[50] To the extent that Francis resembles this psychiatrist, he can believe wholeheartedly in a literal Satan without abandoning his scientific modernity.

Although the pope still presents a curious entanglement of perspectives, it seems fair to conclude that Francis the Old may not be incompatible with Francis the New. Perhaps his new and old passions, for all their apparent differences, serve a single, driving purpose: to challenge the complacency of the contemporary Catholic establishment. New Francis brings liberal economics and the science of climate change to unsettle those who, trusting in Providence, passively accept the status quo. Old Francis revives Satan to rattle those who complacently trust the received world as a product of rational design. This pope says, No!—the Devil has a hand in shaping this world, including its socioeconomic and ecclesiastical structures. Francis the New links with Francis the Old, whatever the resulting embarrassments and awkwardness, to do battle against Catholic complacency.

Chapter 6

The Seven Deadly Sins

Summa Theologica *Meets* Scientific American

Some people have proposed updating the traditional deadly sins to provide a more useful list for contemporary society: replace antique terms like wrath and lust, for example, and focus instead on road rage and sexting. But these proposals miss an important point. The medieval seven sins can accommodate perfectly well all the twists of contemporary vice. Analyzed over centuries by theologians, the ancient sins prove wonderfully complex and flexible as vehicles for understanding the most urgent dangers lurking in human behavior. The old consequences of sinning always included eternal damnation, of course, whereas the new ones may threaten only secular health, happiness, and success; but diagnoses and therapies, now heavily influenced by cognitive science, loom just as important now as they did back in the time of Thomas Aquinas.

Aquinas's *Summa Theologica*, written from 1265 to 1274, represents the most comprehensive attempt by an intellectual Christian to survey the accumulated wisdom of church teachings about every important topic, including the deadly sins. The *Summa* remains one of the most influential resources for Christian theology. In the nineteenth century, in a time of theological ferment, Pope Leo

XIII called for a revival of Aquinas; and after a brief decline in his influence following Vatican II, John Paul II similarly encouraged theologians to reread and give careful attention to Aquinas's work. No single resource within contemporary cognitive science carries similar weight, and of course research and results are ongoing and in flux. A recent issue of *Scientific American*, however, provides a useful window onto contemporary cognitive science as it takes on subjects relevant to the deadly sins. In the seven articles from *Scientific American*, scientists and science writers survey current projects connected with a particular sin. As will become clear in the following comparative analyses of *Summa Theologica* and *Scientific American*, the old and new analyses of deadly sins entangle more compellingly than one might have thought.

AQUINAS AND COGNITIVE SCIENCE: THE ARISTOTLE CONNECTION

In order to provide a foundation for the specific analyses of deadly sins to follow, I would first like to examine, in more general matters of principle and approach, how contemporary cognitive science connects with Aquinas's moral philosophy. Perhaps the best way to understand the entanglement of Aquinas and cognitive science is through their mutual indebtedness to Aristotle.

Aristotle's influence on Aquinas was nowhere more apparent than in matters of ethics. According to Ralph McInerny in *Ethica Thomistica*, Aquinas closely followed Aristotle's lead: "Thomas held that some such account as Aristotle had given captures basic naturally knowable truths about the nature of the good human life."[1] Aristotle and Aquinas share many assumptions and emphases in their thinking about right and wrong behavior. Aristotle posited that the essential human quality is reasoning. The proper measure of a good life, therefore, is how well someone uses reason in making decisions. As he sorted out patterns of good decisions, Aristotle emphasized the ability to navigate between extremes and find a rational middle ground. Eating too much, or eating too little, will ultimately diminish someone's well-being; acting too bravely (taking foolish risks), or not bravely enough (lapsing into cowardice), similarly leads to unhappy results. For Aristotle, the ultimate human goal is *eudaimonia*. This word has traditionally been translated as "happiness," but many modern philosophers prefer "well-being" or "flourishing" as a better indicator of what Aristotle meant. A person who consistently makes properly rational decisions will achieve eudaimonia. Such a person is said to possess "virtue" and "character" and serves as a model to others. Aristotle's ethics, to summarize, are eudaimonistic, virtue-based, and centered in rational avoidance of extremes.

Aquinas's moral philosophy shares these key elements with Aristotle: it derives from eudaimonism, emphasizes virtue (for Aquinas as for Aristotle, a habit of mind that leads to making good decisions), and always looks for the rational middle ground. McInerny explains Aquinas's Christian adaptation of eudaimonia: "There is one single ultimate human good that provides an ordering of all other human goods as partial in relation to it, namely, happiness or better in the Latin *beatitudo*."[2] If Aquinas does not simply duplicate his mentor's ethical philosophy—he discusses specific virtues and vices not found in Aristotle, and depends on Christian revelation to define ultimate happiness in the afterlife—he largely borrows Aristotelian principles of right and wrong behavior.

If cognitive science does not follow Aristotle as closely as Aquinas did, Aristotelian ideas are surprisingly prominent in psychological and neurobiological analyses of morality. A recent MIT collection of essays by cognitive scientists, *Moral Psychology, Volume 5: Virtue and Character*, reveals the persisting relevance of Aristotle. Valerie Tiberius notes that her particular approach ends up "closer to Aristotle" than one might have expected. "This is as it should be," she adds. "Philosophical theories that have withstood the test of time have got something right."[3] In another essay, Kristjan Kristjansson describes himself as "an Aristotelian realist about value," and he cites Martin Seligman's book *Flourish* as an indication that his views are common: "Mainstream positive psychology seems to be taking an objectivist turn by drawing, to a greater extent than before, on Aristotelian insights."[4] Eranda Jayawickreme and William Fleeson remind contemporary scientists that their "interest in virtue ethics," which has "increased dramatically over the last 40 years," retains strong connections to Aristotle that should not be neglected.[5]

The Aristotelian influence common to Aquinas and cognitive science can help bring into focus two important themes of entanglement between medieval theology and contemporary studies of brain and behavior. One theme has to do with the status of reason as the foundation of decision-making. For Aquinas, as for Aristotle, virtue and vice reside in a person's effective or faulty use of reason. Experiments in cognitive science have raised doubts about the role reason plays in decisions about how to act. According to Regina A. Rini in her comprehensive essay on "Morality and Cognitive Science," for a century or so "psychologists have placed much less emphasis on the role of reasoning in moral character."[6] These doubts about reason are due to several factors, including the importance of heuristics (mental shortcuts), the effects of extrarational framing conditions (such as the way a question is worded), and unconscious influences charted by brain MRIs. Some cognitive scientists have gone further than others in dethroning reason. Joshua Greene's MRI results indicated that "deontological" moral claims (normative and rule-based) emerge from the emotional rather than the rational sites of the brain.[7] Jonathan Haidt has argued that moral judgments arrive in flashes of intuition; in his model, as Rini summarizes, "reasoning is only something done post hoc, to rationalize the already-made judgments."[8]

The role of reason remains highly debatable within experimental psychology, but science has raised significant doubts about the reasoning process that Aquinas and Aristotle considered essential to defining virtue and vice. This debate about reason, I would argue, reveals entanglement rather than simple opposition between old and new. Aquinas and Aristotle both worried about elements of emotion that seemed to circumvent or preempt reason, and render the subject not really "free" and morally responsible. (See, for example, the analysis of sloth below.) Granted, they wrote about "passions" rather than "neurotransmitters," but their concern over extrarational determinants links them with cognitive scientists still struggling with those problems.

A second theme of entanglement resides in the distinction between "is-claims" and "ought-claims." Is-claims provide the sort of descriptive information familiar to neuroscience: this anterior location in the brain shows greater activity when a subject is performing a particular task. Ought-claims are the stuff of moral prescription: they tell us which action is preferable in any given situation. Aristotle did his best to manage a distinctive combination of empiricism and normative ethics, which he passed along to Aquinas. The is-ought problem has become more obviously vexing for contemporary cognitive science. As Rini summarizes recent developments among theorists, some "have sought to immunize moral inquiry from empirical revision"—in other words, they keep ought-claims separate from is-claims—while others "have enthusiastically taken up psychological tools to make new moral arguments."[9]

Many philosophers and scientists find themselves somewhere between these two positions. On the one hand, experiments in cognitive science can offer is-claims about the neurological origins of ought-claims. Greene's MRI observations about deontological ethics, for example, tell us something about what sort of cognitive acts these are, and may affect our judgment about their reliability. On the other hand, notes Rini, many philosophers accept the view that "empirical psychology cannot generate moral conclusions *entirely* on its own. . . . Any revision of our moral judgments will be authorized only by some other moral judgments, not by the science itself."[10]

As will become evident in the following analyses of Aquinas and cognitive science, the scientists—for all their experimental sophistication and apparent moral neutrality—find themselves entangled with the older moral judgments set out in the *Summa*. Their analyses of the deadly sins often default to one or another set of prescriptive claims. In the *Scientific American* essay about envy, for example, the underlying moral paradigm aligns with a capitalist set of values. The essay on greed, by contrast, frames its scientific work with anticapitalist assumptions about how humans ought to behave. Unable to wall itself off from moral judgment, *Scientific American* communicates with *Summa Theologica* as a ghostly entangled partner.

SLOTH

When most modern people look over the roster of the seven deadly sins, they likely view sloth as a trivial, almost humorous addition. Sloth means snoozing a few extra minutes, putting off raking the leaves, or sliding away from tax forms to Instagram. All of these may mildly hinder the pursuit of certain goals, but by no means do they indicate the presence of a soul-destroying poison. Slothful people are harmless, often amusing. No one fears a slothful person the way one does a wrathful or envious or greedy villain.

Sloth in its proper medieval sense constitutes a much more serious threat to human lives. The Latin word "acedia" often used in connection with this sin suggests its somber, darker implications. Acedia comes from Greek roots meaning a lack of care. Someone afflicted with acedia has lost interest in the goals and activities of life. They doubt their competence and worth; they become listless, disaffected, bored. Ultimately an acedic soul loses interest in spiritual as well as worldly matters. The medieval sense of sloth as acedia translates perfectly well into modern terms. The diagnosis of "depression" indicates a state of mind with many of the fundamental features of acedia. And although secular doctors do not expect their depressed patients to end up in hell, the therapies they offer have urgent, sometimes life-or-death importance.

In addressing the subject of sloth, Aquinas as usual poses the question of whether sloth should even be considered a sin. The ultimate answer will be "yes," of course, but before he gets there he entertains a plausible objection. The objection comes from Aristotle, whom he honors throughout the *Summa* by referring to him as "the Philosopher." Whenever the Philosopher has written something that seems to conflict with Christian doctrine, Aquinas takes the problem seriously and does his best to resolve it. Aristotle refused to count as a vice any human behavior that was not the product of rational choice. If emotional pressures in someone preempted reason, that person could not be held ethically responsible. As Aquinas notes, "For we are neither praised nor blamed for our passions, according to the Philosopher." He continues, "Now sloth is a passion, since it is a kind of sorrow"; therefore, according to Aristotle's logic, sloth cannot be considered a sin, let alone a deadly one.[11]

Aquinas will eventually turn the argument the other way. But a few passages in the *Summa* suggest that Aquinas appreciated the force of the Philosopher's approach. At one point when he is defining the nature of sloth, he describes it in terms that resonate with Aristotle's idea of sloth as a passion. "The fact that a man deems an arduous good impossible to obtain," he begins, "is due to his being over downcast, because when this state of mind dominates his affections, it seems to him that he will never be able to rise to any good. And since sloth is a sadness that casts down the spirit, in this way despair is born of sloth."[12] The slothful person has been "dominated" by a force that weighs down the spirit. There is no mention of reason as an agent here. The "downcast" soul sounds close enough to a modern diagnosis of depression. Although Aquinas could not have anticipated the degree to which cognitive science now attributes depressive symptoms to imbalanced brain chemistry, he did know the Greek theory of humors—those rough-hewn precursors of neurotransmitters. At one point during his discussion of sloth, Aquinas alludes to the paradigm of humors: "Sloth . . . is an oppressive sorrow, which, to wit, so weighs upon a man's mind, that he wants to do nothing; thus acid things are also cold."[13] The Greek fourfold cosmic scheme includes the "flavor" of "sour" and the "quality" of "cold" under the same rubric: sour/acid and cold both align with the element of Earth. Evidently Aquinas did not shy away from juxtaposing sin and chemistry.

As often happens in the *Summa*, Aquinas shifts course when he announces the primacy of a sacred text. Revelation always trumps the Philosopher. "Whatever is forbidden in Holy Writ is a sin. Now such is sloth, for it is written: 'Bow down thy shoulder, and bear her,' namely spiritual wisdom, 'and not be grieved with her bands' [Ecclesiastes]. Therefore sloth is a sin."[14] The case closes abruptly. Aquinas does attempt to adapt Aristotle's argument so that it fits with Christian truth. "Passions are not sinful in themselves," he says in concession to the Philosopher, "but they are blameworthy in so far as they are applied to something evil. . . . It is in this sense that sloth is said to be a sin."[15] In separating the "passion" from the "application," he posits the coexistence of insuperable emotion—a force that dominates and preempts reason—and rational decision-making. The distinction is philosophically questionable, to be sure, but Aquinas needs something like it to make Aristotle compatible with Christianity.

Contemporary cognitive scientists have no trouble positing that sloth has neurochemical causes. They have no Holy Writ to answer to, no a priori obligation to view sloth as a bad choice by sinful humans. Studies of people prone to procrastination show that they tend to suffer from depression and anxiety. Postponing or avoiding altogether a worrisome task reroutes the brain chemicals to produce a version of pleasure: "Recent research suggests that feeling insecure or gloomy can make us more likely to procrastinate because yielding to our impulses offers an emotional boost."[16]

For all its sophistication, the scientific work on sloth leaves hints of a deeply inscribed Christian structure. Sandra Upson, who wrote the *Scientific American* essay, says the people must learn to "dodge temptations" if they want to overcome slothful habits.[17] Later she summarizes the results of recent studies: "Ultimately, it seems the key is not to constantly fight temptations but to learn to avoid as many of them as possible."[18] All this talk of temptation aligns nicely with Aquinas's Christian model. The scientific conclusions recall key phrases in two prayers. "Lead us not into temptation," says the Lord's Prayer; in the Catholic Act of Contrition, penitents pledge to "avoid the near occasions of sin." Both religion and science call for circumventing temptation rather than confronting and conquering it. The goal for Aquinas's Christians was to achieve "the good" and thereby earn salvation. Science secularizes and leaves indefinite the comparable goal to be earned in defeating sloth. Those who do so will successfully "chase bigger, bolder dreams" and better focus on "what matters in life."[19] Although what matters is unspecified, the ethical structure mirrors Christianity: avoiding sin brings an absolute benefit.

One of the key strategies uncovered by scientists who study sloth is called "cognitive reappraisal." Cognitive reappraisal means that a slothful person manages to rethink a dreaded task so that it becomes more attractive. In one study, for example, students were asked to memorize details about many wines (as they sat in a room full of potential distractions). One group was told simply to do their best; the other group was told that this exercise would strengthen their memory and help them in college. The latter group significantly outperformed the former. The term cognitive reappraisal may be new, but the therapeutic strategy is not. Aquinas for one knew about it and recommended it. He believed the main problem with slothful people came from downcast spirits that dominated thoughts and left room for nothing good. As a remedy, he prescribed cognitive reappraisal, medieval-style. When dealing with some sins, Aquinas advised, people should try to resist them with thoughts that "diminish the incentive to sin, which incentive arises from some trivial consideration. This is the case with sloth, because the more we think about spiritual goods, the more pleasing they become to us, and forthwith sloth dies away."[20]

GLUTTONY

Like sloth, gluttony is usually dismissed as one of the lesser deadly sins—and even more than sloth, gluttony seems to lend itself to comedy rather than tragedy. Gluttonous fictional characters from earlier as well as modern literature generally produce comic effects. Chaucer's Prioress, Shakespeare's Falstaff, Hunter S. Thompson's Dr. Gonzo, to name a few: all gluttons, all comic. Gluttony does have its dark side, though, both in medieval and modern contexts. Medieval theologians worried about near-idolatrous distraction from spiritual goals. (Less gravely, monks eating communally must have chafed when one of them took more than his due.) Modern culture has managed to demonize overeating for different reasons, as Francine Prose makes clear: "Most recently, our fixation on health, our quasi-obscene fascination with illness and death, and our fond, impossible hope that diet and exercise will enable us to live forever have demonized eating in general and overeating in particular."[21]

Gluttony turns out to be a tricky sin for Aquinas. He explains its mortal dangers but shows signs of leniency and toleration. The definition of gluttony is fairly straightforward for him, and it fits well with Aristotle's emphasis on virtuous moderation. "Gluttony denotes, not any desire of eating and drinking," Aquinas begins, "but an inordinate desire. Now desire is said to be inordinate through leaving the order of reason, wherein the good of moral virtue consists."[22] Reasonable eaters and drinkers respect the distinction between necessity and pleasure. Necessity governs the world of "natural appetite" and the "vegetal soul"; here "virtue and vice are impossible, since they cannot be subject to reason." Pleasure emanates from the "sensitive appetite," which brings rational choice back into play, and therefore virtue and vice. "It is in the concupiscence of this appetite that the vice of gluttony consists."[23] Gluttony is not always a mortal sin, says Aquinas, but "if the inordinate concupiscence in gluttony be found to turn many away from the last end, gluttony will be a mortal sin."[24]

Despite its gravity, Aquinas seems inclined toward leniency in the matter of gluttony. He finds an ally in Augustine, who similarly normalized and (to some degree) excused the sin. Aquinas quotes from the *Confessions*: "Who is it, Lord, that does not eat a little more than necessary?"[25] Images of Aquinas suggest he was on the portly side. His colleagues nicknamed the young Thomas "dumb ox," which may have partly reflected his size (and appetite?). In the *Summa*, he leaves hints that with gluttony we should not judge ourselves too strictly. The gravity of gluttony must be tempered due to practical considerations: "The gravity of a sin depends on the person who sins, and from this point of view the sin of gluttony is diminished rather than aggravated, both on account of the necessity of taking food, and on account of the difficulty of proper discretion and moderation in such matters."[26] It is hard to make decisions at the dinner table, in other words. A monk looks at the platter and thinks, do I need a second hunk of roast chicken, or do I just want it? I do feel what I would call hunger, but I also recall how delicious it was and feel drawn to repeat the pleasure. Natural or sensitive appetite? Aquinas acknowledges how difficult it can be to apply the ethical distinctions he explained so clearly. He refers a few times to the pleasures of eating, mentions in an aside that "it does one good to vomit after eating too much,"[27] and generally leans toward discounting most gluttonous acts as venial sins.

In fact, our contemporary culture seems to take gluttony more seriously than Aquinas did. The secular goals become fitness and longevity rather than eternal salvation, but people monitor their eating (and judge other people's eating) with an attentiveness that can border on obsession. The contrary "sins" of obesity and anorexia shock normative standards. Scientists acknowledge, as Aquinas did, that our eating decisions are not always subject to rational control. They often belong to what Aquinas called the "vegetal" realm of subterranean forces. "It turns out that every decision we make about eating," says *Scientific American,* "is influenced by mental and physiological forces that are often outside of our awareness and control."[28] Like Aquinas, scientists nevertheless push forward with normative standards, implying that we can summon enough control to make virtue and vice relevant.

Much of the current scientific work related to gluttony turns on the same question Aquinas laid out: at any given moment, are we eating from necessity or for pleasure? The Aristotelian and scholastic distinction survives intact within modern research laboratories. One of the neuroscientists quoted by *Scientific American* summarizes her approach: "We don't want people to not eat; we want them to not eat just for pleasure."[29] Author Karen Schrock Simring adds, "The way a particular food looks, tastes and feels in our mouth can trick our brain into eating well past necessity."[30] Neuroscientists invoke "necessity" and "pleasure" as if they had lifted them straight from the *Summa.* Many researchers have raised the stakes for gluttony by suggesting that pleasure-based overeating constitutes a kind of addiction. Simring explains, "New research is revealing that those occasional bouts of overeating and eating for pleasure, rather than out of hunger, can push us further down the path to gluttony, priming our brain to want that hedonistic experience more and more. Humans who overeat may develop the same patterns of neural activity in areas of the brain associated with rewarding experiences as drug addicts do."[31]

Addiction is a recent term, of course, and unfamiliar to Aquinas. The equivalent concept for him would be gluttony in its mortal form: impulses so strong that they pull a person away from "the last end" of achieving salvation. In secular rhetoric, the difference between occasional excess and addictive overeating parallels the medieval distinction between venial and mortal gluttony. If Aquinas found it difficult to sort out when he was eating from need and when for pleasure, he managed to exonerate himself from the mortal sin that moderns call addiction.

LUST

If Aquinas showed signs of vulnerability to gluttony, the same cannot be said of lust. A story about the nineteen-year-old Thomas suggests he had little trouble resisting lust. His family, unhappy with his decision to enter the Dominican order, detained him for a year inside the ancestral castle. At one point his brothers hired a prostitute to seduce him. Legend has it that Aquinas chased her out, brandishing a hot iron from the fireplace.

His reflections in the *Summa* indicate a harsher position on lust than on gluttony, the other sin most involved with fleshly appetites. Like gluttony, lust connects with a natural necessity—the perpetuation of humanity—but that fact does little to moderate Aquinas's severity. Some of his predecessors were much more lenient, including Pope Gregory, who drew up the current list of seven deadly sins. Gregory treated lust as the least grave of the seven, because it least offended against the primary virtue of love. Aquinas by contrast offers little in the way of mitigation. He chooses quotations from sacred authorities that roundly condemn lust. From Augustine he selects, "I consider that nothing so casts down the manly mind from its height as the fondling of a woman, and those bodily contacts."[32] Aristotle also provides some help: venereal pleasure proves so absorbing that "it is incompatible with the act of understanding."[33] Aquinas echoes their criticism. Lust "applies chiefly to venereal pleasures, which more than anything else work the greatest havoc in a man's mind"; hence "there is the greatest necessity for observing the order of reason in this matter."[34] Aquinas concedes that venereal acts are necessary for (and only for) reproductive purposes. But that does not deter him from looking down on sexually active humans as almost a lesser species. Even if it is done properly and in keeping with reason, "[s]exual intercourse casts down the mind ... from the height, i.e. the perfection of virtue." Susanna's "conjugal chastity" may be praiseworthy, "yet we prefer the good of the widow Anna, and much more that of the Virgin Mary."[35]

A curious problem edges into Aquinas's remarks on lust. He notes that every vice must have an opposite vice; for lust, this opposite vice is something called "insensibility." Insensibility "occurs in one who has such a dislike for sexual intercourse as not to pay the marriage debt."[36] Aquinas says he thinks few men suffer from lust's contrary defect, and he pays little attention to it: he seems happy to move to another subject. This seems a shame, because it raises an interesting question with respect to the virtuous avoidance of sexual intercourse—namely, the prized state of lifelong virginity. Can we cleanly separate the virtue from the vice? A modern reader might plausibly wonder whether sometimes the "perfection" of virginity shares roots with the "vice" of insensibility.

Scientific American has a much easier time dealing with issues surrounding insensibility (although that medieval term has been replaced by various modern diagnoses). One of the studies it discusses explores the causes of "anorgasmia," the inability to experience orgasm. Cindy Meston of the Sexual Psychophysiology Lab at the University of Texas suggests that too heavy a dose of the frontal lobe may be a key to the problem: "You may not get to the high level of arousal needed for orgasm if you are paying attention to what you look like, or how you measure up to past partners, or what's happening in your relationship instead of what you're actually feeling and experiencing during sex."[37] Aquinas had urged everyone to regulate venereal activities with the careful use of reason, that quintessential frontal lobe activity. If Meston is right, the *Summa* may have discouraged quite a few medieval orgasms.

A different brain study offers some support for Aquinas's views on lust. The *Summa* refers to a contest between the "lower powers" of lust and the "higher powers" of reason. *Scientific American* provides a detailed map of the brain with "lust" areas marked in purple and "love" areas in red. MRI images indicate that lust tends to light up "posterior" areas of the brain, whereas love resides more in the "anterior" areas.[38] MRI delivers something like a literal confirmation of Aquinas's figurative distinction. The agreement between science and *Summa* only goes so far, however. Brain locations for lust and love do not separate quite so neatly. Studies have shown "a more complex and synergistic connection between lust and love." Although lust is associated with the posterior brain, "as lust progresses to love, activity cascades from the back of the insula to the front, with the pleasing sensations of lust (sparked at the back) joined by the abstract feelings of affection (triggered at the front). A similar pattern for lust and love emerges in the striatum, this time traveling from bottom to top."[39] Stephanie and John Cacioppo, the neuroscientists who wrote the *Scientific American* article, name a very different sort of "perfection" with respect to human sexuality: not pious celibacy, but "passionate love." "The strongest relationship— passionate love—involves activation of the home bases of both love and lust."[40] Lesser relationships are common and normal, if less than ideal. Graphed according to their love and lust values, "companionate marriages" mean high love and low lust, "acquaintanceships" a moderate amount of both, and "one-night stands" high lust and low love.[41]

Here the contrast between science and the *Summa* seems most striking. Aquinas would classify one-night stands as mortal sins of either seduction or adultery. In the world of the *Summa*, they show lust at its damnable worst. *Scientific American* treats them with cheerful toleration. "For any two individuals," write the Cacioppos, "the strongest relationship is not necessarily the best outcome: some couplings are just meant to be one-night stands."[42] If neuroscience to some degree confirms the high-low status of love and lust, it also liberates the latter from its moral dungeon.

WRATH

The next two deadly sins differ notably in emphasis from the previous two. As Aquinas remarks on several occasions through the *Summa*, a deadly sin must have a "most desirable end" at its core; otherwise, it would not constitute such a threat. The desirable ends for both gluttony and lust consist of obvious fleshly pleasures. Wrath and envy, by contrast, seem like no fun at all. Their primary motives involve discontent and negative reaction. Both sins do offer compelling goods, however, and wrath and envy are no less dangerous than those sins with more obvious pleasures. Pope Gregory listed them below only pride as potential causes of damnation.

Aquinas makes it clear that wrath has a desirable end. Deployed properly and rationally, it serves a noble purpose in human relations. He uses the term "revenge" without its modern pejorative implication to describe this noble purpose. Revenge is the "appetible object to which anger tends."[43] "If one desire revenge to be taken in accordance with the order of reason, the desire of anger is praiseworthy, and is called 'zealous anger.' "[44] Wrath accords with reason if a person uses it for its "due end, namely the maintenance of justice and the correction of defaults."[45] Wrath is the virtue/vice of authority figures, whether at home, in the monastery, or the larger civic polity.

Someone deploying wrath for a just purpose might still tilt toward sin if the "mode" of anger overreaches propriety: "the movement of anger should not be immoderately fierce, neither internally nor externally; and if this condition be disregarded, anger will not lack sin, even though just vengeance be desired." Wrath also becomes a sin if a person "desire the punishment of one who has not deserved it, or beyond his deserts."[46]

Aquinas follows Aristotle in distinguishing three species of troublesome wrath: "choleric," "stern," and "sullen." Choleric people have a temperament that inclines them to wrathful expression beyond reasonable measure. Choleric sinners become "angry too quickly and for any slight cause." Those whom he describes as stern burn with an "intense desire for revenge, so that it does not wear out with time, and can be quelled only by revenge."[47] Stern avengers do not leave themselves open to rational mitigation of their passion. Finally, sinful wrath may take the form of sullenness. Someone subject to sullen wrath experiences the longest lasting form of the passion: "A sullen person has an abiding anger on account of an abiding displeasure, which he holds locked in his breast; and as he does not break forth into the outward signs of anger, others cannot reason him out of it, nor does he of his own accord lay aside his anger."[48] The sullen sinner craves revenge but cannot or will not act on that craving. Even if the anger began with a reasonable cause, sullenness can turn it into a very dangerous flaw: in such a condition the soul becomes distracted from its primary Christian goal of loving God and neighbor.

It is this sullen soul, as we shall see, that reaches into the future to raise a difficulty for the optimistic psychologists who wrote the wrath article in *Scientific American*. Eli J. Finkel and Caitlin W. Duffy focus their research on incidents of wrathful violence in relationships. The most dramatic of such incidents they classify as "intimate terrorism," when men do serious damage to their partners in an attempt to confirm power and control. (They mention examples from popular culture, including Ike and Tina Turner.) Aquinas would view the Ike Turners of the world as severely choleric, and no doubt he would condemn their wrathful behavior as having neither a reasonable end nor an appropriate mode. But intimate terrorism is fairly rare, according to Finkel and Duffy. Their particular interest lies in "situational couple violence," a far more common form of the problem. "Ten to twenty percent of married couples experience situational violence annually," a recent study found, "and rates are even higher among dating and cohabiting couples."[49]

Finkel and Duffy have done a number of experiments designed to analyze situational couple violence. The causes lie in the "inherent tension present in intimate relationships"—in other words, the irritations, disappointments, and emotional wounds that seem inevitable when two people share so much and depend on each other. Such tensions cause anger and "trigger an urge to lash out."[50] Much of their research explores what they consider the best remedy: self-control. People will not act on their urges to lash out if they have sufficient "self-control—that is, the general ability to work toward goals (for instance, adhering to personal standards of civility or maintaining a good relationship) when those goals conflict with a desire to do something else (such as throw a punch)."[51] Factors that weaken self-control include alcohol consumption, stress, lack of sleep, and various forms of distraction. The psychologists' goal is to find strategies for people to strengthen their self-control as a reliable tonic for wrathful urges. Crucial to their approach is an assumption that couples fundamentally disapprove of their own violent impulses. Finkel and Duffy suggest that "violence in relationships is more akin to a mistake, such as having unprotected sex, breaking your diet or drunk-dialing your ex—that is, an impulse you wish you had suppressed rather than something you believe is okay."[52]

For *Scientific American*, then, wrathful urges are mistakes, and self-control can quell them with happy results. A look back at the *Summa* complicates this therapeutic paradigm. Aquinas did not believe that a wrathful urge was always a mistake. When it emanates from a reasonable desire to correct fault, wrath serves a just, helpful function. If one of Finkel and Duffy's subjects felt that her partner had treated her unjustly, she might not so easily slide away from her angry impulse: she feels a palpable need to correct a fault. Furthermore, the proposed remedy of self-control raises the specter of sullenness, that slow-burning resentment that Aquinas reckoned among the graver dangers of wrath. If our subject still harbors a grievance after she deploys self-control, she may well let it fester as an "abiding displeasure, which [she] holds locked in the heart." It is certainly possible, after all, to be *too* good at self-control. The more modern term would be repression, but sullenness will do. And anything that impinges on "love of neighbor" does damage that rings as true for the modern world as it did for the medieval.

ENVY

Envy was the last of the deadly sins to be codified. Evagrius Ponticus did not include it on his fourth-century list (although he had the other six). The omission is understandable: envy, even less fun than wrath, could be dismissed as a sour concomitant of pride. Gregory not only added envy, however, but placed it just below pride as the most dangerous of sins. In Aquinas's discussion of wrath, at one point he compared wrath with envy, both of which "desire the evil of our neighbor." Aquinas went on to remark that envy is a "more grievous" sin than wrath because it does not carry the noble purpose of justice and correction.[53]

Aquinas includes several quotations from Aristotle and sacred authorities as he conducts his analysis of envy. The basic definition is agreed upon by all: envy means "sorrow for another's good."[54] From there things get more complicated. As will be the case in *Scientific American*, the *Summa* treats envy as having two versions, one helpful and the other dangerous. It is not always so clear how to distinguish the one from the other. For the good version of envy, Aquinas finds support in a passage from one of St. Jerome's letters. A woman has asked Jerome for advice on raising her daughter to become a model of piety. As Aquinas notes, "Jerome says to Laeta about the education of her daughter: 'Let her have companions, so that she may learn together with them, envy them, and be nettled when they are praised.'"[55] Envy thus situated becomes a spur to personal development, as it motivates a person to emulate virtue. Aquinas also turns to Aristotle for something that the Philosopher calls "zeal." "We may grieve over another's good," Aquinas writes, "not because he has it, but because the good which he has, we have not; and this, properly speaking, is zeal, as the Philosopher says."[56] The Greek word *zelos*, which originates in the root for water boiling over, has both a positive and a negative sense. It means an excited state of mind, a noble enthusiasm for someone or something; but it also means a state of envy and contentiousness (hence "jealous" deriving from "zealous"). The Greek word conveniently points in two directions with regard to the sin under discussion. Aquinas reinforces the positive sense with a scriptural quotation: "And if this zeal be about virtuous goods, it is praiseworthy, according to 1 Corinthians 14.1: 'Be zealous for spiritual gifts.'"[57]

Aquinas spends more time with the negative sense of the Greek zeal, the one that aligns with sinful envy. Here he can cite Aristotle comfortably: with the vice of envy, philosophy and theology agree perfectly. "We grieve over a man's good, in so far as his good surpasses ours; this is envy properly speaking, and is always sinful, as also the Philosopher states, because to do so is to grieve over what should make us rejoice, viz. over our neighbor's good."[58] Aquinas goes on to explain why envy amounts to such a grave sin. The greatest of spiritual qualities is charity, "and envy according to the aspect of its object is contrary to charity, whence the soul derives its spiritual life. . . . Charity rejoices in our neighbor's good, while envy grieves over it." He also mentions another anticharity feature of envy—envy's one grim pleasure, schadenfreude—that finds "joy in another's misfortune."[59]

Social psychologists Jan Crusius and Thomas Mussweiler, who wrote the *Scientific American* article on envy, define its two-sidedness very much as the *Summa* did. "In its familiar sinister form," which they label "malicious," "envy can lead us to harm others and even take pleasure in their suffering." The positive version, "benign envy," "can motivate us to try harder and perform better on challenging tasks."[60] They do not mention the ambiguity of the Greek word for zeal, but they note that in some modern languages, two different words convey these different senses of envy.

Unlike Aquinas, Crusius and Mussweiler emphasize the positive, motivational aspect of envy. Their experiments imply that the most valued outcomes have to do with *success* rather than *virtue*. They connect their work with some other researchers who study envy from an evolutionary perspective. These researchers suggest that "repeatedly comparing ourselves with our neighbors could have helped us assess how we were faring in the competition for resources. Furthermore, the frustration and feelings of inferiority ignited by envy can act as a warning signal that alerts us to disadvantage."[61] Evolution may have hardwired us for envy. As in all such arguments, the definition of success reduces to reproductive benefit; the moral concerns that Aquinas held paramount are bracketed as irrelevant for the purposes of this strictly evolutionary analysis. Both the *Summa* and *Scientific American* speak of "neighbors," but in the first case they are to be loved, and in the second to be bested as competitors. Crusius and Mussweiler also imply that economic success is the ultimate goal of benign envy. Among its other consequences, they say, is that "[e]nvy can also exaggerate desires. If a neighbor buys a luxury car, for example, we may suddenly find ourselves toying with the same idea."[62] "Exaggerated desires" for worldly possessions always alarmed Aquinas, but in *Scientific American*, this is a good outcome because it drives markets. The psychologists similarly emphasize economic success when they use "productivity" as the key result of channeling envy. As people pursue their "goals" and "game plans," the once sinister force can serve as an ally: benign envy is "the more productive of its two forms," "the more productive cousin."[63]

Curiously, Crusius and Mussweiler conclude their article with a sentiment as traditional as John Milton's theology (and to the modern ear, as corny as a Hallmark card). Amid all their amoral evolutionary and economic values, they offer something like "count your blessings." "If envy fails to fuel your motivation," they write, "try invoking a sense of gratitude instead. Dwelling not on what we lack but on all that we have can help us value our own numerous boons and lucky breaks."[64] Milton similarly corrected Satan, the original deadly sinner, who let envy displace gratitude.

GREED

The scientists who wrote the greed article in *Scientific American*, unlike their counterparts for envy, challenge the underlying assumptions and goals of capitalist competition. In this respect they join with Aquinas, who steadfastly opposed usury, even as European Christendom was gradually shifting to an economic paradigm that depended on for-profit lending. Both the *Summa* and this piece from *Scientific American* go against the grain of contemporary thinking about markets and consumption.

Aquinas's emphasis in his analysis of greed is not so much usury, because laws had effectively quantified what constitutes sinful lending. When it comes to personal decisions and behavior, greed poses more difficult questions. And the stakes are high: St. Paul memorably claimed that "the desire of money is the root of all evil." Aquinas quotes Paul and then elaborates: "Accordingly, we must say that covetousness [our translators' preferred synonym for greed], as denoting a special sin, is called the root of all sins, in likeness to a tree, in furnishing sustenance to the whole tree. For we see that by riches man acquires the means of committing any sin whatever, and of sating his desire for any sin whatever."[65] Beyond abetting the personal sins of an individual, greed also represents a sin "directly against one's neighbor."[66] Riches disproportionately amassed by one person will deprive others of their due. Some of the worst offenders are misers, who have such a strong "internal affection" for money that they "love and delight in them" beyond any practical value.[67]

Aquinas's brief definition of greed sounds simple enough: "the immoderate desire for riches."[68] As was the case with gluttony, however, it can be difficult to tell the difference between what we need and what we want. We all need a certain amount of money to live normal lives, but our desires may lead us into excessive accumulation of wealth. Aquinas describes a person's desire for riches as moderate and proper "in so far as they are necessary for him to live in keeping with his condition of life."[69] Unfortunately, this formula offers little help to Christians examining their consciences for signs of greed. "Condition of life," an ambiguous term, allows too much interpretive leeway for someone prone to self-justification—or for that matter, to self-blame.

Although Aquinas cannot deliver much practical advice for those trying to distinguish between immoderate desire for riches and a sensible need for them, he does diagnose an unexpected symptom of greed that might help expose it. This unpleasant condition he calls "restlessness." People properly acquire riches, he argues, with the goal of attaining "happiness or felicity, which is the last end of human life." He cites Boethius's remark that riches "give great promise of self-sufficiency." "One of the conditions of happiness is that it be self-sufficing," Aquinas continues, "else it would not set man's appetite at rest." The virtuous management of wealth conduces to felicity and a feeling of satisfaction. Sinful greed, by contrast, "gives rise to restlessness, by hindering man with excessive anxiety and care, for 'a covetous man shall not be satisfied with money' [Ecclesiastes]."[70] Far from putting our appetites to rest, greed excites them beyond any means of satisfaction.

Behavioral economists Dan Ariely and Aline Gruneisen will support this medieval diagnosis of restlessness with data from modern experiments. Essentially, they apply psychological research methods to questions of economic values and decisions. One of their conclusions resonates with Aquinas's warning about greed's paradoxical unhappiness: "Yet if you are still trying to surpass the Joneses, bear in mind that above the poverty line, having more money will not make you appreciably happier. In fact, research shows that individuals who focus on financial success are less stable and less happy overall."[71] Three elements of their summary connect back to the *Summa*. First, "restlessness" finds a modern translation as "less stable and less happy." Second, Aquinas noted that the greedy often show an inordinate interest in riches for their own sake; Ariely and Gruneisen similarly describe "individuals who focus on financial success," presumably instead of focusing on other, warmer human ends. Finally, *Scientific American* supplements the *Summa* with something more specific in the way of a "need" versus "want" distinction. Ariely and Gruneisen implicitly define need as an income above the poverty line, the minimum amount of resources that will allow someone access to happiness. Beyond that, they claim, accumulation of wealth will not generate the expected return in happiness, and may well cause instability and discontent.

In other parts of the article, they provide more detail about the mechanisms of greedy unhappiness. Those who immoderately focus on economic gain suffer from the harmful side effects of "corrosive competition." Ariely and Gruneisen use the example of athletic competition, where the most successful participants "may not spend enough time with their friends and families, or they may sacrifice their long-term health to perform better in the short term—by overexerting their body or taking performance-enhancing drugs such as steroids."[72] Another problem emanating from a greedy distortion of values lies in "expenditure cascades," a term they borrow from Cornell economist Robert H. Frank. Expenditure cascades occur when "high spending by top earners shifts the reference point for those earning just a bit less, affecting those next in the ladder of prosperity, and so on. This chain of events can culminate in all classes spending more than they can afford, leading to a higher likelihood of bankruptcy, divorce, and longer commutes to work."[73] Even outside the explicit context of Christian morality—where "the desire for money is the root all evil"—science seeks and finds secular punishments for bad behavior.

PRIDE

Most Christian theologians, including Aquinas, consider pride the deadliest of the deadly sins. Greed qualifies as the root of all evil because accumulated riches can nourish the indulgence of all other sins, but pride "is said to be 'the beginning of all sins' . . . because any kind of sin is naturally liable to arise from pride."[74] A story from the end of Aquinas's life suggests that he took a drastic measure to fend off this most fundamental of sins. In 1273, with much but not all of the *Summa* written, he suddenly abandoned the project. Reginald of Piperno noticed that his friend had put away his writing tools, which worried him; he and everyone else around had only known Aquinas as a man totally absorbed in his writing. Might he soon resume his work? "I cannot," Thomas replied, "for everything I have written seems to me like straw."[75] He never wrote again. Whatever else might have been going on in his mind (or body) at the time— some speculate that a mystical vision came upon him, others a health crisis—it seems a fair guess that he was repudiating the pride he must have felt in writing such a book.

Two ideas from the *Summa* help explain the unique danger and gravity of pride. Unlike the other six vices, pride is often hidden from the sinner. People guilty of pride can believe in their own excellence so wholeheartedly that they recognize no fault. Aquinas remarks that God in his mercy may allow a proud person "to fall into other sins" that have more obvious symptoms—lust or gluttony, for example—in order to stimulate much-needed repentance. (He compares this process to a physician inducing a lesser disease to prevent a more serious one.[76]) Besides being dangerously hidden, pride has another distinction among the deadly sins. Aquinas quotes Boethius to make the key point: "While all vices flee from God, pride alone withstands God."[77] The mortally proud do not fear divine justice. They imitate Satan in defying subjection to God. Pride in this sense can be seen, from a Christian standpoint, as the root of secularity and atheism.

As one would expect with a sin defined as "an immoderate desire of one's own excellence," pride also has strong connections with virtue.[78] Aquinas recalls Gregory's point that "sometimes a man is elated by sublime and heavenly virtues."[79] He also quotes Jerome: "There is a good and an evil pride . . . a sinful pride which God resists, and a pride that denotes the glory which he bestows."[80] Aquinas reminds us that humans were made in "God's image and likeness"; this fact justifies reasonable aspirations for excellence.[81] Pride has a contrary vice, moreover, which Aquinas calls "pusillanimity" (a term borrowed from Aristotle).[82] Pusillanimous people think so little of themselves that they invite sloth and despair. A dose of the good sort of pride, the kind that disdains neither God nor neighbor, counteracts pusillanimous impulses. Even when Aquinas refers to pride as "self-love," there is a good version as well as a bad one: "Well ordered self-love, whereby man desires a fitting good for himself, is right and natural."[83]

The "fitting goods" stimulated by "well ordered" pride may seem obvious enough examples of virtue. Indeed, *Scientific American* will confidently distinguish between good and bad pride based on motives and deeds. As a prelude to that scientific analysis, however, we should pay heed to a warning embedded in the *Summa*. Aquinas notes that "it is difficult to avoid pride, since it takes occasion even from good deeds." He quotes Augustine, who "says pointedly that [pride] 'lies in wait for good deeds.'" Pride will come "creeping in secretly" when humans are most vulnerable, the very time they feel confident they have acted with virtuous excellence.[84] From a spiritual perspective, in other words, when life looks like easy street, there is danger at your door—in the form of the gravest and best camouflaged sin.

Scientific American joins the *Summa* in identifying a good and a bad pride. Psychologist Jessica Tracy calls the former "authentic pride" and the latter "hubristic pride." Her definition of pride has a more psychological emphasis than the one given by Aquinas: "Pride is a pleasurable emotion that arises when people feel good about themselves; it can bring out both the best and the worst in human nature."[85] Tracy like Aquinas recognizes the unique gravity of pride, but she does not attend to the way "the worst" can creep in disguised as "the best."

Tracy and her collaborator Richard W. Robins "discovered in a series of psychological studies [that] people can feel pride in two very different ways." Authentic pride "motivates hard work and creative thinking"; authentically proud people feel "self-esteem" and earn "prestige" as leaders.[86] Hubristically proud people also are motivated to succeed and become leaders, but they achieve high status through intimidation and bullying. Deep down they feel "insecurity" rather than "self-esteem," and their elevated position is best described as "dominant" rather than "prestigious."[87] Psychological experiments indicate that people recognize and react differently to these two types.

The experimental results may look clear enough, but a problem arises within the *Scientific American* article. When Tracy introduces the two types of pride, she uses an example for each that muddies the distinction between good and bad. Her example for authentic pride is Mark Zuckerberg, in real life and as portrayed in the book *The Accidental Billionaires* and the movie *The Social Network*. Zuckerberg is anything but a clear-cut example of the good sort of pride. As Tracy says later in her article, hubristic pride "can cost friendships, relationships, and even mental health."[88] Zuckerberg's pride (entwined with envy) ruined his relationship with his best friend, Eduardo Savarin. This is not to say that Zuckerberg is a clear example of hubristic pride, either; he has pursued noble philanthropic ends and earned prestige as a cultural leader. Tracy's example for hubristic pride is just as confusing: she names Muhammad Ali. Although Ali offers some of the features of bad pride—she cites the arrogance of "I Am the Greatest!"—surely this man is too complex to serve as a clean example. Ali was arrogant but playfully so, taunted opponents but showed generosity, seemed self-absorbed but selflessly inspired political change. Did Tracy simply choose two unfortunate examples? Perhaps, but the problem may lie deeper: pride, as Aquinas knew, hides its nature better than any other sin. That fact should give pause to anyone who draws a bright line of distinction between good and bad versions of it.

The most provocative element of Tracy's research appears near the end of her article. It turns out that the good type of pride and the bad type work equally well as strategies for success: "In short, dominance, just like prestige, helps us get our way and influence others. . . . Like it or not, it pays to be a bully and not only in a prison or schoolyard—even in a group of high-achieving college students trying to solve a puzzle."[89] From a strictly secular, evolutionary perspective, no particular advantage attaches to authentic over hubristic pride. Interestingly, however, Tracy concludes her discussion by recuperating moral rectitude. Hubristic pride works, "but that doesn't mean [it] is a good idea." Authentic pride needs to be "sought and nourished." It "makes us care whether we are good, hard-working people—pushing us to sign up for volunteer activities, for example."[90] This contemporary scientist, in other words, finds herself entangled with Aquinas in all his normative confidence. Inside the imposing secularity of an academic psychology lab, she defends a model of good behavior that owes as much to doctrine as to experiment.

Chapter 7

Psychedelic Last Rites

The Roman Catholic sacrament known as extreme unction (more familiarly called last rites, or anointing of the sick) presents something of a paradox as a Christian signifier. For Catholics, it means a salvific event of great importance: it brings conclusive intervention by the Holy Ghost in order to render a dying person's soul fit for heaven. Extreme unction enables a "supernatural invigoration of the soul" that will allow the dying person to "repel the assaults of the tempter in what is likely to be the last and decisive conflict in the warfare of eternal salvation."[1] But Protestants view extreme unction as a fraud and an embarrassment. The Protestant churches are united in their rejection of what they consider an archaic practice, a pseudosacrament with only the slimmest scriptural authority. Priests bearing oil to the dying, John Calvin writes, do not save souls but "delude" them: these priests "make themselves ridiculous, therefore, by pretending that they are endued with the gift of healing."[2]

It is easy enough to understand Protestant objections to extreme unction. Catholics acknowledge that the sacrament has only one scriptural foundation, a passage from the Epistle of James: "Is any man sick among you? Let him bring in the priests of the church, and let them pray over him, anointing him with oil in the name of the Lord. And the prayer of faith shall save the sick man: and the

Lord shall raise him up: and if he be in sins, they shall be forgiven him" (5:14–15). Calvin makes a plausible and typically Protestant case against the perpetuation of such healing rituals. God permitted these sorts of wonders, he admits, but only for a short time: "The gift of healing disappeared with the other miraculous powers, which the Lord was pleased to give for a time, that it might render the new preaching of the gospel forever wonderful."[3] The implication is that God resorted to such blunt instruments of persuasion reluctantly, and only to give the new church a decisive start. Conversion achieved by supernatural display is less mature and substantive than that which comes from enlightened reflection. Calvin ridicules priests' claims that the oil they apply carries sacramental efficacy. The apostles used oil as a symbolic mediation, he argues, to make it clear that the healing power did not come directly from them, but from the Holy Ghost. Although those days of regular miraculous intervention are long gone, Catholic priests continue to cherish their oils as if they were magical potions: "These men deign not to use any oil but that which has been consecrated by a bishop, that is warmed with much breath, charmed by much muttering, and saluted nine times on bended knee. Thrice Hail, holy oil! Thrice Hail, holy chrism! Thrice Hail, holy balsam!"[4] Calvin's contempt was no doubt aggravated by reports of extortion; like many other Catholic instruments of salvation, extreme unction was vulnerable to abuse associated with clerical venality.

A secular counterpart of extreme unction has emerged within the world of psychedelic drug research. Back in the 1960s, doctors and scientists began to explore whether drugs like LSD, usually in conjunction with some version of psychotherapy, can alleviate the anxiety and depression afflicting patients with terminal cancer. Might the mental alterations caused by psychedelics so radically reorient consciousness that death would no longer frighten? Might a new sense of cosmic identity transform the ordinary ego and thereby revitalize a patient's spirits?

Although results showed real promise, all such research ended when LSD and other psychedelics were made illegal. Lawmakers designated them "Schedule I" drugs, on the premise that they had "no currently accepted medical use and a high potential for abuse." Recently, however, doctors and scientists have received limited approval for resuming these experimental trials. Once again, early results look promising. But psychedelic therapy for the dying is vulnerable to debunking for reasons that are comparable to doubts raised about its ancient cousin, extreme unction. For some, psychedelic therapy is the closest secular equivalent to a sacrament, and delivers a genuine salvific experience; for others, it offers at best a simulation of religious enlightenment, and at worst a kind of pseudospiritual coercion. As we shall see, psychedelic therapy for the dying has connections with all three supposed effects of extreme unction, as well as the doubts and reservations that surround them.

THE CASE FOR EXTREME UNCTION

In sorting through the various issues surrounding extreme unction, I have found it most helpful to rely on Father Patrick Toner's excellent essay on the subject in *The Catholic Encyclopedia*, written early in the twentieth century. Toner cites the most important statements from ecclesiastical documents through Christian history, and draws on a thorough, influential essay written in Latin a few years earlier by Jesuit Joseph Kern. Current church practice calls for the administration of the sacrament to any Catholic who is suffering an illness grave enough that death seems the probable outcome. In the twelfth and thirteenth centuries, for various reasons, the Church upheld a stricter standard for proximity to death; but the practice in earlier centuries, like the modern one, does not restrict the sacrament to those in their very last moments of life. "In cases of lingering disease," most notably cancer, "once the danger has become really serious, extreme unction may be validly administered even though in all human probability the patient will live for a considerable time, say several months."[5] The prerequisite conditions for extreme unction thereby resemble those for psychedelic experimental trials. Modern Catholic doctrine recognizes three effects emanating from extreme unction: actual healing of the body (so that the recipient recovers from the illness); the remission of sins; and an influx of grace that perfects the health of the soul. Of these three, the last is considered the primary, essential effect, although all three remain valid.

Catholics consider the healing of the body to be a genuine but very rare consequence of the sacrament. They cannot simply dismiss this most archaic of the effects—and the one most easily ridiculed by Protestants—but they minimize its significance. When the Council of Trent set out the three effects of extreme unction, they emphasized how the sacrament "strengthens the soul" and "blots out the sins" of the sick person. Then they added as a postscript the more contingent matter of bodily healing: "and sometimes, when it is expedient for his soul's salvation, [it] recovers bodily health."[6]

Catholic theologians have had trouble explaining what it might mean for healing to be "expedient for his soul's salvation." They do not dispute the validity of the effect, to be sure, which is "vouched for by the witness of experience in past ages and in our own day." Some take an apophatic approach and defer to the inscrutability of divine motives: we simply cannot understand why God heals a few who receive last rites. At the other extreme, some have suggested more confidently that God saves the occasional person because "a longer life will lead to a greater degree of glory." Whatever its merits as a practical apology, this idea invites too close an alliance with pre-destination to earn mainstream approval. A compromise approach cites not future benefits but "present spiritual advantage" for the recipient of healing.[7]

In addition to the "why" question of bodily healing, theologians have entertained the "how" question. Again, the simplest approach is apophatic: we have no way of knowing. In other discussions, however, a link is made between the body's healing and the psy-chological benefits emanating from an influx of grace. Toner makes the point clearly: "The fortifying of the soul by manifold graces, by which over-anxious fears are banished, and a general feeling of com-fort and courage . . . reacts as a natural consequence on the physical condition of the patient, and this reaction is sometimes the factor that decides the issue of certain diseases."[8] This explanation makes the most sense from a secular perspective. Doctors sometimes refer to "faith cures" when prayer or sacrament brings a deep calm that has therapeutic effects. But Catholic theologians reject the sugges-tion that extreme unction may amount to a placebo, bereft of super-natural content. Such explanations annoy the faithful as much as they gratify materialists. For Catholics, any physical changes pro-ceed from spiritual effects that are "strictly supernatural." However they happen, and why, these episodes of bodily healing are excep-tions and must not be considered the heart of the sacrament.

The second effect of extreme unction, remission of the patient's sins, appears to be a better candidate for the sacrament's primary purpose. It has clear scriptural authority, it makes good theological sense, and it occurs in all cases for faithful subjects. Catholic doc-trine holds that extreme unction blots out both venial and mortal sins. The tricky part of this effect has to do with a separate sacra-ment, penance, which governs the remission of sins in the ordi-nary course of a Catholic's life. Catholics regularly examine their consciences and confess their sins in order to receive absolution. Ideally, a dying person will be conscious for extreme unction and make a confession before the anointing; both sacraments thereby come into play, and there is no need to worry about the relationship between them. But it is not unusual for someone to receive last rites in a state of unconsciousness (or severely diminished mental capability). How can the sacrament authentically forgive all sins in those cases?

Church thinking on this question has become rather complicated. "There is *per se* a grave obligation imposed by divine law of confessing all mortal sins committed after baptism and obtaining absolution from them," Toner writes, but if a dying person cannot confess and receive penance, it "is not so clear" whether he or she must achieve perfect contrition.[9] (Perfect contrition is motivated by love for God, rather than something less meritorious, such as fear of bad outcomes.) Strict interpreters insist on perfect contrition, but others assume that exceptions can be made. A dying Catholic unable to confess may only need a lesser sort of contrition, "habitual attrition," which means that he or she has experienced at some moment "an act of sorrow or detestation for sins committed."[10] The anointing would then remit all sins, venial and mortal, and save the person from damnation.

The subtlety of this terminology—especially "habitual attrition," an awkwardly scholastic phrase—suggests some dissonance in Catholic thinking. The whole point of the examination of conscience and confession is that forgiveness of sins does not come as a magic stroke from on high: it is earned by acts of substantive reflection and remorse. To the extent that extreme unction might seem to eliminate the need for such acts, it becomes more vulnerable to Calvin's charges of mystification. A comparable issue will become evident in psychedelic therapy for the dying.

Catholic theologians agree that the primary, indisputable effect of extreme unction is the healing of the soul. It is also the effect most clearly comparable to the purpose of psychedelic therapy. According to Toner, Kern makes a definitive case "that the end of extreme unction is the perfect healing of the soul with a view to its immediate entry into glory."[11] The healing comes from a sacramental influx of grace. Both the cause of the healing—grace—and its result, eternal salvation, only have meaning as supernatural events. As theologians elucidate the healing delivered by the sacrament, however, they use terminology more easily understood as natural psychological effects. The Council of Trent explains that extreme unction "alleviates and strengthens the soul of the sick person, by exciting in him a great confidence in the Divine mercy, sustained by which he bears more lightly the troubles and sufferings of disease." Emphasis falls on a psychological effect, confidence, that diminishes the patient's stress and discomfort. Toner echoes this sentiment: postsacramental confidence "will enable him patiently and even cheerfully to bear the pains and worries of sickness."[12] Another apologist itemizes these "pains and worries" as "unruly passions, temptations, fear, diffidence, anxiety, distrust, and depression."[13] These symptoms match up well with those of cancer patients chosen for psychedelic therapy. Diagnoses of anxiety and depression will draw particular emphasis in the psychedelic trials, as a new cohort of secular priests seek out sufferers to whom they will bring their therapeutic "oil."

EARLY PSYCHEDELIC EXPERIMENTS

The connection between dying and the psychedelic experience goes back at least as far as Timothy Leary. In collaboration with Richard Alpert and Ralph Metzner, he published *The Psychedelic*

Experience: A Manual Based on the Tibetan Book of the Dead (1964). *The Tibetan Book of the Dead* amounts to a Buddhist handbook for the administration of something like last rites. The lama reads to the dying (or just deceased) person a description of the stages he or she will go through from the last moments of life through enlightenment or rebirth. The goal is to help the dying person navigate these transitional moments as effectively as possible, so that at least a favorable rebirth will be achieved. Leary, Alpert, and Metzner adapted the book to provide instructions for people about to take a psychedelic trip. They saw parallels between the book's descriptions of dying and their own experiences with LSD. In both cases of transitional consciousness, a person moves from a normal state of mind to an altered state rich with spiritual promise as well as terror. Leary intends the book to be used by a psychedelic guide—someone with psychedelic experience who acts as a sort of minister to the neophytes.

The Psychedelic Experience does not count as psychedelic therapy for the dying: Leary linked tripping with dying, but only symbolically. Readers of his instructions were assumed to be perfectly healthy. Leary's friend Aldous Huxley, however, made likely the first use of a psychedelic drug to improve the actual process of dying. Huxley, one of the most adventurous and thoughtful early experimenters with psychedelic drugs, had written the influential *The Doors of Perception* after his first trip in the 1950s. On his death bed in 1963, he wrote a note to his wife Laura: "LSD: Try it: Intermuscular: 100 mm." She complied, and later gave a second injection at his request. By her account, he died peacefully a few hours afterward. Huxley's psychedelic death was not a scientific experiment like the trials to come in a few years. Nor can it be considered a sacrament, except in the very loosest sense—it was more a self-devised improvisation. Laura Huxley herself had mixed feelings about LSD in general and about its value as an aid to the dying. She later administered LSD to one other dying person, at his request. "For Aldous, it was very good," she summed up. "For the other person, it wasn't."[14]

Scientific trials testing the efficacy of psychedelic therapy for the dying began in the mid-1960s. This was one of several therapeutic possibilities proposed for LSD and other psychedelics, including treatment of alcoholism, depression, anxiety, obsessive-compulsive disorder, schizophrenia, and autism. Some experimenters preferred a series of lighter chemical doses and a gradual evolution of consciousness to achieve altered behavior; others opted for a single large dose, aiming for a dramatic, transformative psychedelic experience. With either approach, the basic idea was to change a subject's sense of self so fundamentally that he or she would shed old mindsets and patterns of behavior.

In trials involving therapy for the dying, scientists put particular emphasis on the kind of mental transformation akin to mystical experiences. Connections between psychedelics and mystical experience were first tested back in 1962 by Walter Pahnke in his famous Good Friday experiment. Pahnke, working at Harvard under the supervision of Timothy Leary, designed an experiment with two groups of divinity students. One group received a dose of psilocybin before the Good Friday chapel service; the other was given an active placebo (nicotinic acid). Pahnke measured the resultant presence or absence of mystical consciousness by responses to a number of questions, including matters of time and space perception, sense of cosmic unity, feelings of sacredness, and overall mood. Students who took psilocybin showed significantly greater indications of mystical experience than did those in the control group. Rick Doblin went back thirty years later to review Pahnke's methods and check on the subjects' retrospective views of the experience. For the most part, Doblin confirmed the validity of the results, as well as the lasting impact on the subjects who took psilocybin.[15] In 2006, Roland R. Griffiths of John Hopkins designed a similar but more carefully controlled trial. Griffith's title summarizes the bottom-line result: "Psilocybin can occasion mystical-type experiences having substantial and sustained personal meaning and spiritual significance."[16]

Griffiths phrases his results cautiously. Subjects underwent a "mystical-type experience," not "a mystical experience"; and the psychedelic trip "occasions" the experience, not "causes" it. It is no simple matter for scientists to choose appropriate verbs as they analyze the religious implications of dying patients' new perspectives. Does a patient's altered consciousness "resemble" a state of religious enlightenment? "Resemble" works if one wishes to maintain a distinction between traditional religious faith and psychedelic altered consciousness. Put that distinction aside, however, and it makes more sense to say that the psychedelic therapy "initiates" or "engenders" a religious experience. Scientists tend to steer away from this problem, even though it lingers in some of their ambiguous terminology (they often refer, for example, to "psychospiritual effects") and other hedges. Science in these quasi-sacramental experiments always courts but never quite marries religion.

The first to test psychedelics on dying patients was Dr. Eric Kast of Chicago Medical School. In 1966, Kast administered 100 micrograms of LSD to eighty patients who were expected to die from cancer within weeks or a few months. In the journal where he reported his results, Kast more or less apologized for features of his work that might not be viewed as properly scientific. "In dealing with a topic of such finality and depth as death," he began, "it is difficult to follow the usual format of a scientific paper. Of necessity one must treat the material from a more holistic and philosophical standpoint."

He articulated a purpose that sounds as much sacramental as scientific: "The investigations in this paper were designed to make the last months of patients with a terminal illness more meaningful and less distressful."[17] In deference to this mission, he significantly compromised scientific rigor by declining to use a control group. All eighty subjects were given the LSD; he felt he could not ethically deny any of these patients the chance for a more "meaningful" last few weeks or months of life. Kast jeopardized the validity of his work, it seems fair to say, because its sacramental value took precedence over scientific method.

In some ways, Kast treated LSD as a magic oil of the sort ridiculed by Protestant critics of extreme unction. He did not prepare his subjects with preliminary psychotherapeutic conversations—unlike later investigators, who would interview patients about their lives and concerns beforehand. There would be no secular equivalent to the confession that ideally accompanies Catholic last rites. He simply gave his subjects a big dose and hoped for the best. Kast even claimed that LSD functioned as a pain reliever that was more effective than the standard analgesics given to cancer patients. In this sense, the LSD trip had a "healing" aspect loosely comparable to the rare physical recovery Catholics still attribute to extreme unction. Pain relief is not exactly healing, of course, and Kast offered no detailed explanation for this effect; but it certainly added to the drug's mystique. This was all happening in 1966, a year before the Summer of Love and a time when Leary and Kesey celebrated LSD as a modern elixir. Kast sounded like an acid enthusiast when he looked forward to the drug "increasing the perceptive powers of the dying patient."[18] LSD does all the work, and the subject simply absorbs the benefits.

Kast's statements about the religious implications of his experiment suggest that he was of two minds about this delicate subject.

On the one hand, he worried that an LSD trip might interfere with patients' religious views and unethically disturb their sober convictions. The psychedelic experience he offers "must not tamper with the patient's religious ideas."[19] After the trials were complete, he was happy to report that "only seven patients felt that the experience in some way interfered with the privacy of their religious and philosophical ideas." All seven, he went on to explain, "experienced strong hallucinatory or frightening images," and he terminated their trips after a few hours with thorazine.[20]

Kast's reluctance to interfere with his subjects' religious ideas clashes with another message equally prominent in his article. If he worried about altering their religious beliefs, he contrarily suggested that some such alteration was precisely the point of the experiment. He said that LSD "may enable the patient to penetrate, to some extent, the mysteries of cessation of existence."[21] He cited Huxley's observation in *The Doors of Perception* that psychedelic drugs promote "a feeling of beneficent oneness and 'universal unity.'"[22] It is hard to reconcile these robust metaphysical claims—subjects may penetrate the mysteries of death, and find oneness with the universe—with Kast's squeamishness about religious interference. Indeed, on the same page where he congratulated himself that only seven patients felt the experience had interfered with their religious ideas, he suggested that alteration of religious ideas was a central feature of the results. A "happy, oceanic feeling" soothed many in the group, and "a certain change in philosophical and religious approach to dying took place."[23]

Two things become clear in Kast's report of his experiment: (1) despite his stated unwillingness to tamper with his subjects' religious views, he both expected and welcomed a shift in cosmic perspective with clear religious implications; and (2) his psychedelic enthusiasm led him to overstate the positive results of his trial. The LSD trip created in his patients "a new will to live and a zest for experience which, against a background of dismal darkness and preoccupying fear, produces an exciting and promising outlook." He went on to conclude, "The profound impact of LSD on the dying was impressive."[24] Kast's praise of psychedelic therapy brushed aside some troubling elements of his results, most notably the number of bad trips that patients experienced. "About half of the patients became upset around six hours after administration," he acknowledged, "and the experience was terminated with chlorpromazine [thorazine]."[25] Roughly forty of these people, in other words, found the psychedelic alteration so unpleasant or frightening that they bailed out. As with Laura Huxley's much smaller sample, LSD therapy for the dying worked only half the time. If Kast did not conceal these darker results, he did not account for them sufficiently in his conclusions. And even the most positive shifts in mood and perspective on death were transient in effect, lasting only a few hours to a few days. Kast's psychedelic experiment had unmistakable sacramental intentions but shortchanged his subjects in sacramental value.

Two studies a few years later cited Kast and designed new psychedelic trials for dying cancer patients. The first came from psychologist Gary Fisher of UCLA. Fisher quoted Kast's enthusiastic (if overstated) conclusion about subjects' "new will to live and zest for experience." His approach was more frankly religious than Kast's. He did not worry, as Kast had, about tampering with patients' religious ideas; indeed, he laid out quite explicitly a Buddhist-themed metaphysics that LSD would inspire in the right sort of patients. Not just anyone would do: Fisher screened potential subjects for their "intelligence" and "sophistication" as they contemplated new cosmic perspectives.

Fisher began his article diagnosing America's dysfunctional attitudes about death, especially the "massive denial" exhibited by patients, their families, and their caregivers. Then he offered a description of Buddhist thinking that could serve as a counter-paradigm. If we can find a way to free ourselves from our "skin-encapsulated" identity (the phrase comes from Zen popularizer Allan Watts), we can experience the sort of ego transcendence to which Buddhists aspire. "The problem of physical death," he wrote, "has something to do with our identity and what is considered to be 'me.' When we identify with our 'skin-encapsulated ego,' we naturally face annihilation. When we can identify with something beyond our skin-self, death has a different face."[26] Fisher reinforced this message later in the article: when a dying person achieves an ego-free state, "he develops a new perspective, as it were, of life, and this perspective typically has at its base a profound acceptance of the life constant, change. . . . Sometimes the individual experiences himself simply as part of the life process, as being 'at one.'" The enlightened patient accepts death as "a natural phenomenon of the cycling of life force."[27]

Fisher, like Leary, believed that the psychedelic experience matched up well with Buddhist metaphysics. He promoted an LSD-inspired Buddhist spirituality as a therapeutic alternative to traditional Christianity. This new spirituality, coupled with inten-sive psychotherapy, would transform the dying experience for his subjects. Even more than Kast's, his experiment had a robust sacra-mental purpose. Fisher spent much of his article detailing how the process played out for some of his patients. One of them, a Catholic woman with conflicted feelings about the sacraments of her church, has particular relevance for this discussion, and her case will be addressed in detail later.

Although his emphasis was clearly on religious transformation, Fisher never abandoned the underlying scientific paradigm. Unlike Kast, he used a control group in the trial, with a double-blind setup.

In this respect, he allowed science to trump sacrament. Sometimes in his article a scientific perspective merges with Buddhist spirituality to produce a curious sort of hybrid discourse: "The solution is to identify with the life process—to experience, for instance, our cellular consciousness (awareness of that fantastic neurophysiological activity) and to experience another's cellular consciousness, and on the other extreme, to experience (in Eastern religious terms) the 'void,' the unmanifested energy (the absence of any thing), the source of all life."[28] He preserved a scientific model of cells and neurophysiology amid much fuzzier Eastern metaphysics. Evidently he thought that LSD bridged the two worlds and thereby created better therapy for the dying than the ones currently offered by medical science and traditional Christianity.

A third study from the early research also produced positive results, although the sacramental features of this trial differed in emphasis from both Kast's and Fisher's. Lead investigator was psychiatrist Stanislav Grof of Johns Hopkins. (Grof had taken over from Walter Pahnke of Good Friday fame, after Pahnke died suddenly in 1971.) Grof cited Kast as the pioneer in LSD therapy for the dying, but he sharply distinguished his own methods from Kast's: "Our approach differed considerably from that of Kast, who had administered the LSD as a chemotherapeutic procedure without even forewarning the patients."[29] By invoking "chemotherapy" with its frightening connotations, Grof implicitly criticizes Kast's naive reliance on LSD as a pharmaceutical silver bullet. Kast just administered the drug and looked for signs of Huxley's oceanic bliss. Grof's goal "was to achieve a psychedelic peak experience in the context of brief intensive psychotherapy."[30] For him, genuine transformation could only happen if patients participated as something more than passive receptacles for a chemical.

He selected thirty-one subjects with terminal cancer who were suffering from "pain, depression, anxiety, and psychological isolation."[31] Several potential subjects declined to join the trial because LSD had received such bad publicity in the wake of hippie enthusiasm. The treatment consisted of three stages: "a series of drug-free interviews in which rapport was established and the patient was prepared for the drug session; the psychedelic session itself; and several subsequent drug-free interviews for the integration of the session."[32] In bracketing the LSD trip with "drug-free" events, Grof clearly wished to de-emphasize the drug as a magic elixir, and to focus primarily on the psychotherapeutic work it facilitated. LSD was more or less the "matter" of this quasi-sacrament—like the oil in extreme unction—rather than the essence of it. The first and third stages of his treatment offered patients a secular version of confession. Just as a Catholic priest strongly prefers that the oil of extreme unction be buttressed by a good confession, Grof wanted psychotherapeutic conversation to confirm and elaborate the drug experience. His "confessional" conversations included "unresolved issues between the patient and family members," as well as "significant intrapsychic conflicts that became evident as the therapeutic relationship developed."[33]

Grof's methods gave his work a more traditional sacramental feel. Furthermore, his experiment generally treated Western religious paradigms with more deference than had some of his psychedelic colleagues. His approach differed notably from Fisher's explicit endorsement of Buddhist alternative spirituality. Grof carefully catalogued the religious affiliations of all thirty-one subjects, all of them Judeo-Christian: sixteen were Jewish, fourteen Protestant, and one Catholic. Although he did not express Kast's worry about tampering with their religious ideas, he recorded and left intact their traditional religious identities; and unlike Fisher, he did not impose a Buddhist template on the results. This is not to say that Grof de-emphasized the religious elements of psychedelic therapy.

He recognized that "increased acceptance of death usually followed sessions in which the patients reported deep religious and mystical experiences."[34] But as Grof described the religious content of such experiences, his account mixed religious themes: "It has been our impression that the most dramatic therapeutic changes followed sessions in which the patient achieved an intense psychedelic peak experience—an experience of unity, usually preceded by agony and death and followed by spiritual rebirth."[35] "Unity" brings to mind the familiar psychedelic Buddhism, while "agony and death" and "spiritual rebirth" lend themselves readily to Christian adaptation.

MORE RECENT PSYCHEDELIC EXPERIMENTS

Grof's report would be the last for a long time. Decades passed before scientists regained permission and funding for psychedelic trials. First to launch new experiments in therapy for the dying was psychiatrist Charles S. Grob of the Harbor-UCLA Medical Center. Grob decided to use psilocybin instead of LSD, in part because "it carries less political baggage and consequently has a far less sensationalized reputation."[36] He doubtless knew that many of Grof's patients had declined to participate from fear of LSD; he also knew how stressful the LSD trips had been for many of Kast's subjects, and psilocybin has a reputation as a gentler drug.

Although he chose a different psychedelic than his predecessors from the 1960s, he followed their lead in emphasizing the therapeutic value of mystical experiences. He cited Griffiths' 2006 study as evidence that "psilocybin could reliably catalyze mystical experiences in prepared subjects."[37] And Grob was the first of these scientists to hint at a connection between his work and old-school sacraments for the dying: "Huxley, according to his closest colleagues, often said that 'the last rites should make one more conscious rather than less conscious, more human rather than less human.' "[38] Like most of his predecessors, Grob gave all of his subjects a chance to try the active psychedelic, thereby letting sacramental purpose infringe on scientific rigor in the design of the study. Grob justified his decision on ethical grounds but offered a kind of apology to scientists: his method has "inherent limitations," and "a better experimental design might incorporate an independent control group."[39] Perhaps more than any other investigator, Grob found himself performing a balancing act between the roles of priest and scientist. The priest offered psilocybin to everyone; the scientist regretted the suboptimal experimental design. The priest wrote of "transcendent mystical states" and "epiphanies"; the scientist attended to evidence of "metabolic hyperfrontality [that] may be related to states of ego disintegration and derealization phenomena."[40] ("Hyperfrontality" refers to an emerging theory of how psychedelic drugs work: serotonin-based chemical effects overwhelm frontal areas of the brain, so that the brain's normal processes of communication and integration break down.)

In both of the articles where he discusses his work, Grob leaned on the ambiguous term "psychospiritual" as a way of managing the tensions between religious and scientific paradigms. He called for "the judicious use of hallucinogens with patients in profound psychospiritual crisis. Indeed, such treatment may be considered as existential medicine designed to directly intervene and ameliorate the emotional and spiritual suffering of dying patients."[41] Set aside for a moment the more secular terms in his hybrid vocabulary—"psychological" and "emotional"—and the statement sounds close enough to a description of extreme unction. The primary effect of Catholic last rites was to invigorate the soul, thereby repelling the tempter and easing a person's last moments on earth. Psychedelic therapy will "ameliorate" the suffering of a cancer patient who is facing "spiritual crisis." But Grob preferred to use "spiritual" only in tandem with "psycho-." It gave him a hedge against too close an alignment with the sacramental. His ambiguous compound adjective allows a secular reader to attribute putative spiritual content to psychological causes. Elsewhere Grob referred to patients' "psychospiritual distress"[42] and the "psychospiritual epiphanies"[43] that would comfort them. Both the underlying problem and its solution may be characterized as psychological states—and therefore explainable by scientists strictly as brain chemistry—or as spiritual states, not reducible to materialist analysis.

A current NYU study in psychedelic therapy for the dying, led by psychiatrist Stephen Ross, has received a good deal of attention. The bottom-line result: 80 percent of subjects who received an active dose no longer felt anxious or depressed, compared with 30 percent for the placebo group. Ross and his colleagues have given interviews to several journalists and offered many details. Ross like Grob chose a modest dose of psilocybin, in conjunction with a series of psychotherapeutic sessions. Evidence gathered by journalists suggests that the NYU study positioned itself somewhat uneasily between religious and scientific paradigms. Ross showed real sacramental flair by handing each subject the psilocybin in an ornate chalice. Other religious symbols had a more Eastern than Western cast. In fact, some details suggest that Ross's careful setting for the trips amounted to steering his subjects in the direction of Buddhism. The psilocybin trips took place in "a converted exam room . . . refitted for comfort with holistic panache: plush pillow-strewn sofa, Persian carpet, Buddha statuettes, books on spirituality and mysticism."[44] Another source describes "ethnic-printed pillows, shelves stocked with oversize books of Tibetan art, framed landscape photographs, warm pools of lamplight, Buddha figurines."[45]

The NYU interior decorators obviously knew and encouraged the Leary-influenced history of psychedelic Buddhism. And it would appear that their encouragement worked. Anthony Bossis, one of the investigators, summarized patients' new outlooks in loosely Buddhist terms: "People come out with an acceptance of the cycles of life. We're born, we live, we find meaning, we love, we die, and it's all part of something perfect and fine. The emergent themes are love, and transcending the body in this existence."[46]

Other parts of journalistic accounts indicate that the scientific paradigm held its own against chalices and Buddha statues. Alex Liu gave priority to science over religion after speaking with Ross. "Ultimately, scientists hope these studies will help elucidate the neurobiology of spirituality."[47] From this perspective, science matters more than religion: religion is just one of many natural phenomena that science will eventually explain on its own terms. Many new atheists have proposed evolutionary theories for the development of religious behaviors. Ross himself seems to endorse this line of inquiry: "The fact that we have neural tissue that allow for these experiences shows us that the brain evolved to have spiritual experiences. These agents let us know about different reward pathways other than pleasure."[48]

Journalists who interviewed Ross and his subjects alternately emphasized the science—serotonin receptors, hyperfrontal activity, evolution—and the mystical visions of cosmic oneness. Because they find it difficult to align and compare the two perspectives, they simply juxtapose them. They hedge, in other words, just as Grob hedged with all of his "psychospiritual" descriptions. Alexander Zaitchik in *Salon* offers a typically ambiguous summation: "The palliative-care literature finds that those with a sense of a transcendental force have less depression and anxiety. This can mean belief in a Judeo-Christian god, or a direct memory of the nameless, overwhelming sense of eternal, cosmic love occasioned by the injection of 20 or 30 milligrams of psilocybin."[49] There are really three levels of religious signification here. One reinforces a traditional Christian faith; another suggests a more Eastern mystical state; and the last reduces religion to neurochemistry. Psychedelic therapy welcomes—but does not integrate—all three possibilities.

PSYCHEDELIC CATHOLICS

Mainstream Catholicism flatly rejects any so-called spiritual experience that bears such a tenuous affiliation with "the Judeo-Christian god." Nor would any priest be happy if his parishioner entered a clinical trial that steers patients toward Eastern mysticism. Still, the spiritual claims surrounding psychedelic drugs in the 1960s attracted some faithful Catholics to experiment with what seemed a new sacramental vehicle. According to Jeffrey Kripal, influential theologian John Courtney Murray was "among many Jesuits who experimented with LSD to catalyze their thought, meditation, and artistic endeavors." After one Jesuit took an acid trip at a UCLA clinic, he recalled that "the bed suddenly became the universe, and he, her lover; the two had joined in cosmic bliss. He said the experience left him with a profound sense of the meaning of Christ's becoming embodied."[50] Bestselling nutritionist Adelle Davis, a devout Catholic, took LSD five times under a psychiatrist's supervision. Davis said she took the drug "in hope of overcoming spiritual poverty" and "to get chemical Christianity."[51] She published an account of her psychedelic experiences (under the pseudonym Jane Dunlap), which included visions of Jesus and Buddha. Despite the Church's official disapproval, both Davis and the Jesuits found their psychedelic visions to be compatible with Catholic faith.

Gary Fisher's early clinical trial included an intriguing case study of a dying Catholic, torn between traditional and psychedelic sacrament, who eventually found spiritual peace through psychedelic therapy. This was a forty-five-year-old woman with multiple cancers who suffered from depression. Fisher learned her life story from preliminary interviews. She had stayed for twenty years in a bad marriage because of her strong Catholic faith, but finally got a divorce. When she remarried a few years later, her father disowned her and "she was refused her church sacraments."[52] It was shortly after her second marriage that she learned of the cancer. Facing death, she went to a priest and "attempted to absolve her sins with relation to marrying outside of the Church. She tried to reassure herself that she was not living in sin but obviously had great difficulty believing it."[53] She made a traditional Catholic effort to receive remission of sins, in other words, but it did not work. She suffered from guilt but had no wish to renounce her second, happier marriage. And as long as she was living unrepentant in mortal sin (from the Church's point of view), she could not receive extreme unction.

So she tried Fisher's LSD therapy as an alternative. The 200-microgram dose gave rise to intense psychotherapeutic conversations with investigators. It became clear to them that she associated physical pain with the emotional pain of her father's and the Church's rejection. As she tried to work through the pain, her emotions cycled through guilt, resentment, and anger. A crucial psychedelic moment came as she listened to choral music sung by the choir of Montserrat Cappella. The voices seemed to be attracting her to a sacred place, but she felt they were denying her entry because of her sins. "They don't think I belong in the church. . . . They are pleading, but they won't let me in. Oh, I want in, I want in."[54] The woman eventually resolved her feelings of guilt and rejection by the Church. She began to anticipate death as a "garden" world of freshness and delight: "She said, 'Death is a place you go to rest. It's such a beautiful road. It smells so fresh. Look at the light shining through the trees.'" Now the choral music conveyed a very different message— "the monks have come back and they say everything is going to be all right."[55] Fisher noted that due to her "transcendent experience," "her previous notion and fear that she would burn in the fires of hell no longer held any validity for her."[56] She left the LSD therapy in a composed, peaceful state of mind. Her regular doctor said he had never seen such a dramatic transformation.

Except for the exotic drug that served as "oil," and a substitution of psychiatrist for priest, this woman's story sounds like textbook extreme unction. A distressed, dying Catholic found remission of sins and invigoration of the soul. She bore her last weeks much more cheerfully. Psychedelic enthusiasts would conclude that the new last rites did a splendid job of replacing the old. Mainstream Catholics would counter that the woman's experience was by no means authentically religious or salvific. Although a therapist steered her in the direction of self-forgiveness, she in fact remained sinful. Furthermore, her euphoria was the artificial, temporary product of neurochemical deviation, not a sacramental influx of grace.

Arguments for and against psychedelic last rites are no more easily resolved than the original disputes between Catholics and Protestants over extreme unction. If trials with psilocybin continue to show positive results, however—and if that drug should someday earn legal reclassification—those arguments are likely to take on greater urgency for both the secular and the faithful. Nothing catalyzes an entanglement of religion and secularity like the near prospect of death. It presents to everyone one final, awful psychospiritual challenge, in both the new and the old senses of "awful": causing dread, and worthy of profound respect.

NOTES

Chapter 1

1. All quotations in this and the following paragraph come from Dr. Terry Mortenson, "Young Earth Creationist View Summarized and Defended," *Answers in Genesis*, February 16, 2011. https://answersingenesis.org/.../ young-earth/young-earth-creationist-view-summarized and defended.
2. Christopher Hitchens, *God Is Not Great: How Religion Poisons Everything* (New York: Twelve Books, 2007), 64.
3. Hitchens, *God Is Not Great*, 102.
4. Bill Maher, *Religulous*, directed by Larry Charles (Los Angeles: Lions Gate, 2008), DVD.
5. Robert Barron, quoted in J. Peter Nixon, "Has Hell Frozen Over?," *U.S. Catholic*, November 15, 2011, 13.
6. Stephen Jay Gould, *Rocks of Ages: Science and Religion in the Fullness of Life* (New York: Ballantine, 1999), 54.
7. Gould, *Rocks of Ages*, 56.
8. Gould, *Rocks of Ages*, 54.
9. Leo P. Ribuffo, "Henry Ford and 'The International Jew,'" *American Jewish History* 69 (1980): 455.
10. Claire Conner, *Wrapped in the Flag: A Personal History of America's Radical Right* (Boston: Beacon Press, 2013), 81.
11. Daniel Denvir, "A Short History of the War on Christmas: How Everyone from Bill O'Reilly to Jon Stewart Became a Co-Conspirator in an Annual Farce,"

NOTES

Politico, December 16, 2013. www.politico.com/magazine/story/2013/12/war-on-christmas-short-history.

12. "The Naughty-or-Nice 2016 Retailer List," American Family Association, afa.net. November 30, 2016. www.afa.net/who-we-are/press-releases/2016/11/who-s-naughty-who-s-nice/.

13. Joshua Feuerstein's Facebook page, November 5, 2015. https://www.facebook.com/joshua.feuerstein.5/videos/689569711145714.

14. Peter Montgomery, "Religious Right's Annual War on the 'War on Christmas' Has a New Field Marshal," *Right Wing Watch*, November 17, 2016. www.rightwingwatch.org/.../religious-rights-annual-war-on-the-war-on-christmas-has-a-new-field-marshal.

15. Montgomery, "Religious Right's Annual War."

16. "Quotes on Stem Cell Research," Pew Research Center, July 17, 2008. http://www.pewforum.org/2008/07/17/quotes-on-stem-cell-research-from-political-religious-and-other-prominent-figures.

17. All summaries of religious positions in this paragraph are drawn from "Religious Groups' Official Positions on Stem Cell Research," Pew Research Center, July 17, 2008. www.pewforum.org/2008/.../religious-groups-official-positions-on-stem-cell-research.

18. *Embryonic Stem Cell Research: Exploring the Controversy*, 108th Cong., Senate Hearing 108–958 (September 29, 2004), U.S. Government Printing Office, 8.

19. *Embryonic Stem Cell Research*, 8.

20. *Embryonic Stem Cell Research*, 8.

21. Congressional Record 151, 109th Cong., no. 106: (July 29, 2005). Senate, 2.

22. Congressional Record 151, S9,325 (daily ed. July 29, 2005).

23. Congressional Record 151, S9,325 (daily ed. July 29, 2005).

24. George Jacob Holyoake, *English Secularism: A Confession of Belief* (1896). Project Gutenberg, 2011. http://www.gutenberg.org/ebooks/38104.

25. Louis Menand, "Saved from Drowning: Barthelme Reconsidered," *New Yorker*, February 23, 2009, 68.

26. Talal Asad, *Formations of the Secular: Christianity, Islam, Modernity* (Stanford, CA: Stanford University Press, 2003), 24.

27. Asad, *Formations*, 7.

28. Charles Taylor, *A Secular Age* (Cambridge, MA: Harvard University Press, 2007), 15.

29. Michael Warner, Jonathan VanAntwerpen, and Craig Calhoun, eds., *Varieties of Secularism in a Secular Age* (Cambridge, MA: Harvard University Press, 2010), 7–8.

30. Tracy Fessenden, *Culture and Redemption: Religion, the Secular, and American Literature* (Princeton, NJ: Princeton University Press), 2006.

31. Jacques Berlinerblau, "The Crisis in Secular Studies," *Chronicle of Higher Education*, September 8, 2014. www.chronicle.com/article/The-Crisis-in-Secular-Studies/148599.

Chapter 2

1. Sam Harris, *The End of Faith: Religion, Terror, and the Future of Reason* (New York: Norton, 2004), 333.
2. Gould, *Rocks of Ages*, 41.
3. Harris, *The End of Faith*, 227.
4. Jim Holt, *Why Does the World Exist? An Existential Detective Story* (New York: Liveright, 2012), 125.
5. Holt, *Why Does the World Exist*, 125.
6. Holt, *Why Does the World Exist*, 157.
7. Steven Weinberg, "A Designer Universe," *New York Review of Books*, October 21, 1999, 48.
8. Lawrence M. Krauss, *A Universe from Nothing: Why There Is Something Rather Than Nothing* (New York: Atria, 2012), 174.
9. Krauss, *A Universe from Nothing*, xvi–xvii.
10. Krauss, *A Universe from Nothing*, xvii.
11. Richard Dawkins, *The God Delusion* (Boston: Houghton Mifflin, 2006), 140.
12. Henry Peacham, *The Garden of Eloquence* (1593; repr., Gainesville, FL: Scholars' Facsimiles and Reprints, 1954), S2v.
13. Alain de Botton, *Religion for Atheists: A Non-Believer's Guide to the Uses of Religion* (New York: Vintage, 2012), 11.
14. Daniel C. Dennett, *Breaking the Spell: Religion as a Natural Phenomenon* (New York: Penguin, 2006), 27.
15. Maher, *Religulous*.
16. Richard Sherry and Desiderius Erasmus, *A Treatise of Schemes and Tropes: and His Translation of the Education of Children by Desiderius Erasmus* (1550; repr., Gainesville, FL: Scholars' Facsimiles and Reprints, 1961), 46.
17. Peacham, *The Garden of Eloquence*, S4r.
18. Hitchens, *God Is Not Great*, 64.
19. Hitchens, *God Is Not Great*, 65.
20. Hitchens, *God Is Not Great*, 87.
21. Krauss, *A Universe from Nothing*, xxv.
22. Harris, *The End of Faith*, 73.
23. Hitchens, *God Is Not Great*, 69.
24. De Botton, *Religion for Atheists*, 10.
25. Dawkins, *The God Delusion*, 134, 143, 46, 38.
26. Harris, *The End of Faith*, 19.
27. Dawkins, *The God Delusion*, 56.
28. Dennett, *Breaking the Spell*, 36.
29. Harris, *The End of Faith*, 17.
30. Dawkins, *The God Delusion*, 335.
31. Dennett, *Breaking the Spell*, 36.
32. Harris, *The End of Faith*, 26–27.

33. John Smith, *The Mystery of Rhetoric Unveil'd* (London: printed for Robert Clavel, 1688; Early English Books online). https://quod.lib.umich.edu/e/eebo/A59234.0001.001.
34. Harris, *The End of Faith*, 11.
35. Harris, *The End of Faith*, 227.
36. Dawkins, *The God Delusion*, 117.
37. De Botton, *Religion for Atheists*, 13.
38. De Botton, *Religion for Atheists*, 13–14.
39. Holt, *Why Does the World Exist*, 149.
40. Holt, *Why Does the World Exist*, 150.
41. Holt, *Why Does the World Exist*, 151.
42. Holt, *Why Does the World Exist*, 153.
43. Alan Lightman, *The Accidental Universe: The World You Thought You Knew* (New York: Vintage, 2013), 53.
44. Lightman, *The Accidental Universe*, 53–54.
45. Lightman, *The Accidental Universe*, 44.
46. Harris, *The End of Faith*, 48–49.
47. Smith, *The Mystery of Rhetoric Unveil'd*.
48. Harold Bloom, *A Map of Misreading* (New York: Oxford University Press, 1975), 73.
49. Bloom, *A Map of Misreading*, 74.
50. Harris, *The End of Faith*, 225.
51. Dennett, *Breaking the Spell*, 245.
52. Dennett, *Breaking the Spell*, 244.
53. Hitchens, *God Is Not Great*, 94.
54. Krauss, *A Universe from Nothing*, 178.
55. Lightman, *The Accidental Universe*, 38.
56. Harris, *The End of Faith*, 42.
57. Harris, *The End of Faith*, 20.
58. Krauss, *A Universe from Nothing*, 179–180.
59. Holt, *Why Does the World Exist*, 160.
60. Holt, *Why Does the World Exist*, 160–161.
61. John Milton, *Paradise Lost*, in *John Milton: Complete Poems and Major Prose* (Indianapolis: Odyssey Press, 1957), 212.

Chapter 3

1. Owen Gingerich, *God's Universe* (Cambridge, MA: Harvard University Press, 2006), 5.
2. Gingerich, *God's Universe*, 5–6.
3. John Polkinghorne, *Science and Religion in Quest of Truth* (New Haven, CT: Yale University Press, 2011), 69.

4. Polkinghorne, *Science and Religion*, 22.
5. Francis Collins, *The Language of God: A Scientist Presents Evidence for Belief* (New York: Free Press, 2006), 5.
6. Collins, *The Language of God*, 156.
7. Polkinghorne, *Science and Religion*, 15.
8. Polkinghorne, *Science and Religion*, 73.
9. Collins, *The Language of God*, 29.
10. Collins, *The Language of God*, 29.
11. Collins, *The Language of* God, 140.
12. Collins, *The Language of* God, 140.
13. Gingerich, *God's Universe*, 12; italics added.
14. Gingerich, *God's Universe*, 39; italics added.
15. Gingerich, *God's Universe*, 77; italics added.
16. Gingerich, *God's Universe*, 96; italics added.
17. Gingerich, *God's Universe*, 110; italics added.
18. Gingerich, *God's Universe*, 121.
19. Collins, *The Language of God*, 204.
20. Polkinghorne, *Science and Religion*, 4.
21. Collins, *The Language of God*, 225.
22. Gingerich, *God's Universe*, 96.
23. Collins, *The Language of God*, 36.
24. Polkinghorne, *Science and Religion*, 73.
25. Polkinghorne, *Science and Religion*, 12.
26. Gingerich, *God's Universe*, 59.
27. Gingerich, *God's Universe*, 102.
28. Stephen Jay Gould, *Rocks of Ages: Science and Religion in the Fullness of Life* (New York: Ballantine, 1999).
29. Collins, *The Language of God*, 80.
30. Collins, *The Language of God*, 82.
31. Collins, *The Language of God*, 228.
32. Max Jammer, *Einstein and Religion* (Princeton, NJ: Princeton University Press, 1999), 40.
33. Jammer, *Einstein and Religion*, 40.
34. Jammer, *Einstein and Religion*, 97.
35. Jammer, *Einstein and Religion*, 97.
36. Jammer, *Einstein and Religion*, 27.
37. Jammer, *Einstein and Religion*, 93.
38. Jammer, *Einstein and Religion*, 93.
39. Jammer, *Einstein and Religion*, 144.
40. Jammer, *Einstein and Religion*, 49.
41. Baruch Spinoza, *The Ethics and Selected Letters*, trans. Samuel Shirley (Indianapolis: Hackett, 1982), 154.
42. Jammer, *Einstein and Religion*, 48.

43. Jammer, *Einstein and Religion*, 48.
44. Chris Matyszczyk, "Stephen Hawking Makes It Clear: There Is No God," CNET, September 26, 2014. https://www.cnet.com/news/stephen-hawking-makes-it-clear-there-is-no-god.
45. Collins, *The Language of God*, 62–63.
46. Matyszczyk, "Stephen Hawking Makes It Clear."
47. Collins, *The Language of God*, 75.
48. Stephen Hawking, *A Brief History of Time* (New York: Bantam, 1988), 140–141.
49. Steven Weinberg, *The First Three Minutes: A Modern View of the Origin of the Universe* (Glasgow: William Collins, 1977), 148.
50. Polkinghorne, *Science and Religion*, 106.
51. Polkinghorne, *Science and Religion*, 107.
52. Polkinghorne, *Science and Religion*, 87.
53. Collins, *The Language of God*, 67.
54. Collins, *The Language of God*, 200.
55. Gingerich, *God's Universe*, 69.
56. Collins, *The Language of God*, 63.
57. Collins, *The Language of God*, 18.
58. Polkinghorne, *Science and Religion*, 61.
59. Polkinghorne, *Science and Religion*, 81.
60. Polkinghorne, *Science and Religion*, 73.
61. Gingerich, *God's Universe*, 117.
62. Gingerich, *God's Universe*, 117–118.
63. Collins, *The Language of God*, 44.
64. Collins, *The Language of God*, 44.
65. Collins, *The Language of God*, 46.

Chapter 4

1. M. H. Abrams, ed., *The Norton Anthology of English Literature* (New York: Norton, 1962), 1:xxv.
2. M. H. Abrams, ed., *The Norton Anthology of English Literature*, 3rd ed. (New York: Norton, 1974), 1:xxxi.
3. M. H. Abrams, *The Norton Anthology of English Literature*, 5th ed. (New York: Norton, 1986), 1:xxxvi.
4. Stephen Greenblatt, ed., *The Norton Anthology of English Literature*, 8th ed. (New York: Norton, 2006) 1:xxii.
5. Stephen Greenblatt, ed., *The Norton Anthology of English Literature*, 9th ed. (New York: Norton, 2012), 1:xiii.
6. Abrams, *Norton*, 3rd ed., 1:xxxi.

7. Abrams, *Norton*, 1:xxvi.
8. Abrams, *Norton*, 3rd ed., 1:xxvii.
9. Greenblatt, *Norton*, 9th ed., 1:xxiv.
10. David Damrosch, "The Mirror and the Window: Reflections on Anthology Construction," *Pedagogy* 1 (2001): 210–211.
11. David P. Alvarez, "Reason and Religious Tolerance: Mary Astell's Critique of Shaftesbury," *Eighteenth-Century Studies* 44 (2011): 489–490.
12. Robert M. Adams, in Abrams et al., *Norton*, 1:913.
13. Adams, in Abrams et al., *Norton*, 1:911–912.
14. Adams, in Abrams et al., *Norton*, 1:981.
15. Adams, in Abrams et al., *Norton*, 3rd ed., 1:1156.
16. Adams, in Abrams et al., *Norton*, 5th ed., 1:1555.
17. Barbara K. Lewalski, in M. H. Abrams and Stephen Greenblatt, eds., *The Norton Anthology of English Literature*, 7th ed. (New York: Norton, 2000), 1:1971.
18. Adams, in Abrams et al., *Norton*, 1:920.
19. Adams, in Abrams et al., *Norton*, 3rd ed., 1:1098.
20. Lewalski, in Abrams and Greenblatt, *Norton*, 7th ed., 1:1816.
21. Adams, in Abrams et al., *Norton*, 1:989.
22. Lewalski, in Abrams and Greenblatt, *Norton*, 7th ed., 1:1816.
23. Constance Jordan and Clare Carroll, in *The Longman Anthology of British Literature*, ed. David Damrosch et al. (New York: Longman, 1999), 1:1755.
24. Adams, in Abrams et al., *Norton*, 3rd ed., 1:1661.
25. Adams, in Abrams et al., *Norton*, 5th ed., 1:1751.
26. E. Talbot Donaldson, in Abrams et al., *Norton*, 1:82–83.
27. Alfred David and E. Talbot Donaldson, in Abrams and Greenblatt, *Norton*, 7th ed., 1:216.
28. Alfred David and James Simpson, in Greenblatt et al., *Norton*, 8th ed., 1:220.
29. David and Simpson, in Greenblatt et al., *Norton*, 8th ed., 1:220.
30. Christopher Baswell and Anne Howland Schotter, in Damrosch et al., *Longman*, 1:295.
31. Roy Liuzza et al., eds., *The Broadview Anthology of British Literature* (Peterborough, ON: Broadview Press, 2006), 1:157.
32. David and Simpson, in Greenblatt et al., *Norton*, 8th ed., 1:383.
33. Jon Stallworthy and Jahan Ramazani, in Greenblatt et al., *Norton*, 8th ed., 2:2289.
34. Hallett Smith, in Abrams et al., *Norton*, 1:468.
35. Smith, in Abrams et al., *Norton*, 3rd ed., 1:569.
36. Smith, in Abrams et al., *Norton*, 3rd ed., 1:572.
37. Smith, in Abrams et al., *Norton*, 3rd ed., 1:554.
38. Jordan and Carroll, in Damrosch et al., *Longman*, 1:760.
39. Joseph Black and Anne Lake Prescott, in Liuzza et al., *Broadview*, 5:152.

40. Stephen Greenblatt and George M. Logan, in Abrams and Greenblatt, *Norton*, 7th ed., 1:622.
41. Sean Shesgreen, "Canonizing the Canonizer: A Short History of *The Norton Anthology of English Literature*," *Critical Inquiry* 35 (2009): 311.
42. Jon Stallworthy and David Daiches, in Abrams and Greenblatt, *Norton*, 7th ed., 2:2842.
43. Stallworthy and Ramazani, in Greenblatt et al., *Norton*, 8th ed., 2:2853.
44. Stallworthy and Daiches, in Abrams and Greenblatt, *Norton*, 7th ed., 2:842–843.
45. Salman Rushdie, *The Satanic Verses* (New York: Viking, 1988), 93.
46. I am grateful to my colleague Jeffrey Kenney for his help with this analysis of complications surrounding the name of the Prophet.
47. Stallworthy and Ramazani, in Greenblatt et al., *Norton*, 9th ed., 2:3001.
48. Daiches, in Abrams, *Norton*, 2:1235.
49. George Ford and Carol Christ, in Abrams et al., *Norton*, 5th ed., 2:1579.
50. Daiches, in Abrams et al., *Norton*, 2:1235.
51. Daiches, in Abrams et al., *Norton*, 2:1235.
52. Ford and Christ, in Abrams et al., *Norton*, 5th ed., 2:1581.
53. David E. Anderson, "The Grandeur of God and the Life of the Poet," *Religion and Ethics Newsweekly*, March 20, 2009. Pbs.org/wnet/religionandethics.
54. Harold Bloom, in *The Oxford Anthology of English Literature*, ed. Frank Kermode et al. (New York: Oxford University Press, 1973), 2:1466.
55. Abrams, *Norton*, 3rd ed., 2:368.
56. Abrams, *Norton*, 3rd ed., 2:370.
57. Shesgreen, "Canonizing the Canonizer," 310.
58. Jack Stillinger and Deirdre Lynch, in Greenblatt et al., *Norton*, 8th ed., 2:609.
59. Ford and Christ, in Abrams et al., *Norton*, 5th ed., 2:1548.
60. Heather Henderson and William Sharpe, in Damrosch et al., *Longman*, 2:1778.

Chapter 5

1. Austen Ivereigh, *The Great Reformer: Francis and the Making of a Radical Pope* (New York: Picador, 2014), 35.
2. "Blood of St. Januarius Liquefies during Francis' Visit to Naples," *Catholic Herald*, March 21, 2015. www.catholicherald.co.uk > Latest News.
3. "Blood of St. Januarius."
4. Herbert Thurston, "St. Januarius," in *The Catholic Encyclopedia* (New York: Robert Appleton Company, 1910), accessed in New Advent, November 5, 2016. http://www.newadvent.org/cathen/08295a.htm.
5. Associated Press, "Pope Francis Praises Turin Shroud as an 'Icon of Love,'" *Guardian*, June 21, 2015.

6. Frank Viviano, "Why Shroud of Turin's Secrets Continue to Elude Science," *National Geographic*, April 17, 2015. http://news.nationalgeographic.com/2015/04/150417-shroud-turin-relics-jesus-catholic-church-religion-science/.

7. Viviano, "Shroud of Turin's Secrets."

8. Viviano, "Shroud of Turin's Secrets."

9. Tia Ghose, "Is It a Fake? DNA Testing Deepens Mystery of Shroud of Turin," *Live Science*, October 23, 2015. https://www.livescience.com > Strange News.

10. Nick Squires, "Pope Francis Links Turin Shroud to Jesus Christ," telegraph.co.uk, March 30, 2013. http://www.telegraph.co.uk/news/religion/9962709/Pope-Francis-links-Turin-Shroud-to-Jesus-Christ.

11. Associated Press, "Pope Francis Praises Turin Shroud."

12. Taylor Marshall, "Pope Francis and Popular Devotions," *Taylor Marshall PhD* (blog), May 12, 2014.

13. "Popular Devotional Practices: Basic Questions and Answers," United States Conference of Catholic Bishops, November 12, 2003. www.usccb.org > Prayer and Worship > Prayers and Devotions > Prayers.

14. Herbert Thurston, "Relics," in *The Catholic Encyclopedia*, accessed in New Advent, November 6, 2016. http://www.newadvent.org/cathen/08295a.htm.

15. Thurston, "Relics."

16. Paul Vallely, *Pope Francis: The Struggle for the Soul of Catholicism* (New York: Bloomsbury, 2015), 20.

17. Vallely, *Pope Francis*, 38.

18. Vallely, *Pope Francis*, 39.

19. Vallely, *Pope Francis*, 127.

20. Ivereigh, *The Great Reformer*, 19.

21. Ivereigh, *The Great Reformer*, 19.

22. Vallely, *Pope Francis*, 136.

23. Vallely, *Pope Francis*, 137.

24. William C. Stewart et al., "Review of Clinical Medicine and Religious Practice," *Journal of Religion and Health* 52 (2013): 91.

25. L. Roberts, I. Ahmed, and A. Davison, "Intercessory Prayer for the Alleviation of Ill Health," *Cochrane Database of Systematic Reviews* (2009). www.cochrane.org/.../SCHIZ_intercessory-prayer-for-the-alleviation-of-ill-health.

26. Candy Gunther Brown, *Testing Prayer: Science and Healing* (Cambridge, MA: Harvard University Press, 2012), 274.

27. Brown, *Testing Prayer*, 185.

28. Basak Coruh et al., "Does Religious Activity Improve Health Outcomes? A Critical Review of the Recent Literature," *Explore* 1 (2005): 188.

29. "Putting the Placebo Effect to Work," *Harvard Health Letter*, April 2012. https://www.health.harvard.edu/mind-and-mood/putting-the-placebo-effect-to-work.

30. Cara Feinberg, "The Placebo Phenomenon," *Harvard Magazine,* January/February 2013, 11.
31. Feinberg, "The Placebo Phenomenon," 12.
32. C. S. Lewis, *The Screwtape Letters* (1942; repr., New York: HarperOne, 2015), 3.
33. Gustav Niebuhr, "Is Satan Real? Most People Think Not," *New York Times,* May 10, 1997.
34. Niebuhr, "Is Satan Real?"
35. Gareth Leyshon, "Exorcism and Prayers for Deliverance: A Historical Review of the Developments since the Late Nineteenth Century," June 28, 2016. www.drgareth.info/Deliverance.
36. American Psychiatric Association, *Diagnostic and Statistical Manual of Mental Disorders* (Arllington, VA: American Psychiatric Publishing, 2013), 293–294.
37. Thomas Rosica, "Why Is Pope Francis So Obsessed with the Devil?," CNN.com, July 20, 2015. www.cnn.com/2015/07/20/living/pope-francis-devil/index.html.
38. Peter Stanford, "Exorcism: What Does the Boom in Demand Tell Us about Pope Francis's Catholic Church?," *Independent,* April 14, 2015.
39. Nick Donnelly, "Pope Francis Challenges Priests Who Don't Believe in the Devil or in the Power of Exorcism," *Protect the Pope* (blog), October 13, 2013. protectthepope.com/?p=8672.
40. Stanford, "Exorcism."
41. Leonardo Blair, "Man in Pope Francis Exorcism Story Says He's Still Possessed by Demons," *Christian Post Reporter,* May 31, 2013.
42. Stanford, "Exorcism."
43. Caroline Wyatt, "Pope Francis's Reforms Polarise the Vatican," BBC.com, March 27, 2016. www.bbc.com/news/world-europe-35869656.
44. Rosica, "Why Is Pope Francis So Obsessed."
45. Rosica, "Why Is Pope Francis So Obsessed."
46. Cindy Wooden, "Battle with the Devil: Pope Francis Frames the Fight in Jesuit Terms," *National Catholic Reporter,* April 18, 2013.
47. Andrew Delbanco, *The Death of Satan: How Americans Have Lost the Sense of Evil* (New York: Farrar, Strauss, and Giroux, 1995), 64.
48. Delbanco, *The Death of Satan,* 3.
49. Stephen A. Diamond, "Exorcism as Psychotherapy: A Clinical Psychologist Examines So-Called Demonic Possession," *Psychology Today,* February 5, 2011. https://www.psychologytoday.com/…/exorcism-psychotherapy-clinical-psychologist.
50. Richard Gallagher, "As a Psychiatrist, I Diagnose Mental Illness. Also, I Help Spot Demonic Possession," *Washington Post,* July 1, 2016.

Chapter 6

1. Ralph McInerny, *Ethica Thomistica* (Washington, DC: Catholic University of America Press, 1997), 31.

2. Ralph McInerny and John O'Callaghan, "Saint Thomas Aquinas," in *Stanford Encyclopedia of Philosophy* (Stanford University, 1997). Article published July 12, 1999. Revised May 23, 2014. https://plato.stanford.edu/entries/aquinas.

3. Valerie Tiberius, "Does Virtue Make Us Happy? A New Theory for an Old Question," in *Moral Psychology*, Vol. 5: *Virtue and Character*, ed. Walter Sinnott-Armstrong and Christian B. Miller (Cambridge, MA: MIT Press, 2017), 553.

4. Kristjan Kristjansson, "A Tale of Two Default Approaches: Some Old Answers for a New Theory," in Sinnott-Armstrong and Miller, *Moral Psychology, Volume 5*, 558–559.

5. Eranda Jayawickreme and William Fleeson, "Does Whole Trait Theory Work for the Virtues?," in Sinnott-Armstrong and Miller, *Moral Psychology, Volume 5*, 76.

6. Regina A. Rini, "Morality and Cognitive Science," in *Internet Encyclopedia of Philosophy*, June 30, 2015. www.iep.utm.edu/m-cog-sci.

7. Joshua D. Greene, "The Secret Joke of Kant's Soul," in *Moral Psychology*, Vol. 3: *The Neuroscience of Morality: Emotion, Brain Disorders, and Development*, ed. Walter Sinnott-Armstrong (Cambridge, MA: MIT Press, 2008), 47.

8. Rini, "Morality and Cognitive Science."

9. Rini, "Morality and Cognitive Science."

10. Rini, "Morality and Cognitive Science."

11. Thomas Aquinas, *Summa Theologica*, trans. Fathers of the English Dominican Province (New York: Benziger Brothers, 1947), 2.II.35.1.

12. Aquinas, *Summa*, 2.II.35.4.

13. Aquinas, *Summa*, 2.II.35.1

14. Aquinas, *Summa*, 2.II.35.1

15. Aquinas, *Summa*, 2.II.35.1

16. Sandra Upson, "Prodding Our Inner Sloth," *Scientific American Mind* 24 (2013): 46.

17. Upson, "Prodding Our Inner Sloth," 46.

18. Upson, "Prodding Our Inner Sloth," 49.

19. Upson, "Prodding Our Inner Sloth," 49.

20. Aquinas, *Summa*, 2.II.35.1.

21. Francine Prose, *Gluttony* (New York: Oxford University Press, 2003), 4.

22. Aquinas, *Summa*, 2.II.148.1.

23. Aquinas, *Summa*, 2.II.148.1.

24. Aquinas, *Summa*, 2.II.148.2.

25. Aquinas, *Summa*, 2.II.148.1.

26. Aquinas, *Summa*, 2.II.148.3.
27. Aquinas, *Summa*, 2.II.148.6.
28. Karen Schrock Simring, "Accidental Gluttons," *Scientific American Mind* 24 (2013): 28.
29. Simring, "Accidental Gluttons," 28.
30. Simring, "Accidental Gluttons," 29.
31. Simring, "Accidental Gluttons," 31.
32. Aquinas, *Summa*, 2.II.153.2.
33. Aquinas, *Summa*, 2.II.153.2.
34. Aquinas, *Summa*, 2.II.153.3.
35. Aquinas, *Summa*, 2.II.153.2.
36. Aquinas, *Summa*, 2.II.153.3.
37. Stephanie Cacioppo and John T. Cacioppo, "Lust for Life," *Scientific American Mind* 24 (2013): 62.
38. Cacioppo and Cacioppo, "Lust for Life," 58–59.
39. Cacioppo and Cacioppo, "Lust for Life," 60.
40. Cacioppo and Cacioppo, "Lust for Life," 60.
41. Cacioppo and Cacioppo, "Lust for Life," 60.
42. Cacioppo and Cacioppo, "Lust for Life," 60.
43. Aquinas, *Summa*, 2.II.158.4.
44. Aquinas, *Summa*, 2.II.158.2.
45. Aquinas, *Summa*, 2.II.158.2.
46. Aquinas, *Summa*, 2.II.158.2.
47. Aquinas, *Summa*, 2.II.158.5.
48. Aquinas, *Summa*, 2.II.158.5.
49. Eli J. Finkel and Caitlin W. Duffy, "The Thin Line between Love and Wrath," *Scientific American Mind* 24 (2013): 52.
50. Finkel and Duffy, "The Thin Line," 53.
51. Finkel and Duffy, "The Thin Line," 53.
52. Finkel and Duffy, "The Thin Line," 53.
53. Aquinas, *Summa*, 2.II.158.3.
54. Aquinas, *Summa*, 2.II.36.1.
55. Aquinas, *Summa*, 2.II.36.2.
56. Aquinas, *Summa*, 2.II.36.2.
57. Aquinas, *Summa*, 2.II.36.2.
58. Aquinas, *Summa*, 2.II.36.2.
59. Aquinas, *Summa*, 2.II.36.3.
60. Jan Crusius and Thomas Mussweiler, "Untangling Envy," *Scientific American Mind* 24 (2013): 36.
61. Crusius and Mussweiler, "Untangling Envy," 36.
62. Crusius and Mussweiler, "Untangling Envy," 37.
63. Crusius and Mussweiler, "Untangling Envy," 37.

64. Crusius and Mussweiler, "Untangling Envy," 37.
65. Aquinas, *Summa*, 2.II.118.5.
66. Aquinas, *Summa*, 2.II.118.1.
67. Aquinas, *Summa*, 2.II.118.1.
68. Aquinas, *Summa*, 2.II.118.1.
69. Aquinas, *Summa*, 2.II.118.1.
70. Aquinas, *Summa*, 2.II.118.7.
71. Dan Ariely and Aline Gruneisen, "The Price of Greed," *Scientific American Mind* 24 (2013): 42.
72. Ariely and Gruneisen, "The Price of Greed," 41.
73. Ariely and Gruneisen, "The Price of Greed," 41.
74. Aquinas, *Summa*, 2.II.162.7.
75. Brian Davies, *The Thought of Thomas Aquinas* (Oxford: Oxford University Press, 1993), 9.
76. Aquinas, *Summa*, 2.II.162.6.
77. Aquinas, *Summa*, 2.II.162.6.
78. Aquinas, *Summa*, 2.II.162.2.
79. Aquinas, *Summa*, 2.II.162.5.
80. Aquinas, *Summa*, 2.II.162.1.
81. Aquinas, *Summa*, 2.II.162.1.
82. Aquinas, *Summa*, 2.II.162.1.
83. Aquinas, *Summa*, 2.II.162.8.
84. Aquinas, *Summa*, 2.II.162.6.
85. Jessica L. Tracy, "Pride and Power," *Scientific American Mind* 24 (2013): 66.
86. Tracy, "Pride and Power," 66.
87. Tracy, "Pride and Power," 66.
88. Tracy, "Pride and Power," 68.
89. Tracy, "Pride and Power," 68.
90. Tracy, "Pride and Power," 68.

Chapter 7

1. Patrick Toner, "Extreme Unction," in *The Catholic Encyclopedia* (New York: Robert Appleton Company, 1910), accessed in New Advent. http://www.newadvent.org/cathen/05716a.htm.
2. John Calvin, *The Institutes of the Christian Religion*, trans. Henry Beveridge (Grand Rapids, MI: Christian Classics Ethereal Library, 2002), IV.xix.18.
3. Calvin, *Institutes*, IV.xix.18.
4. Calvin, *Institutes*, IV.xix.18.
5. Toner, "Extreme Unction," 17.
6. Toner, Extreme Unction," 17–18.

7. Toner, "Extreme Unction," 19.
8. Toner, "Extreme Unction," 19.
9. Toner, "Extreme Unction," 18.
10. Toner, "Extreme Unction," 18.
11. Toner, "Extreme Unction," 20.
12. Toner, "Extreme Unction," 19.
13. Winfrid Herbst, *Call the Priest* (St. Louis: Queen's Work, 1952). https://www.ecatholic2000.com/cts/untitled-66.shtml.
14. Wayne Glausser, *Cultural Encyclopedia of LSD* (Jefferson, NC: McFarland, 2011), 83–84.
15. Rick Doblin, "Pahnke's 'Good Friday Experiment': A Long-Term Follow-Up and Methodological Critique," *The Journal of Transpersonal Psychology* 23 (1991): 1–28.
16. R. R. Griffiths et al., "Psilocybin Can Occasion Mystical-Type Experiences Having Substantial and Sustained Personal Meaning and Significance," *Psychopharmacology* 187 (2006): 268.
17. Eric Kast, "LSD and the Dying Patient," *The Chicago Medical School Quarterly* 26 (1966): 80.
18. Kast, "LSD and the Dying Patient," 80.
19. Kast, "LSD and the Dying Patient," 80.
20. Kast, "LSD and the Dying Patient," 86.
21. Kast, "LSD and the Dying Patient," 80.
22. Kast, "LSD and the Dying Patient," 81.
23. Kast, "LSD and the Dying Patient," 86.
24. Kast, "LSD and the Dying Patient," 86–87.
25. Kast, "LSD and the Dying Patient," 82.
26. Gary Fisher, "Psychotherapy for the Dying: Principles and Illustrative Cases with Special Reference to the Use of LSD," *Omega* 1 (1970): 4.
27. Fisher, "Psychotherapy for the Dying," 5.
28. Fisher, "Psychotherapy for the Dying," 4.
29. S. Grof et al., "LSD-Assisted Psychotherapy in Patients with Terminal Cancer," *International Pharmacopsychiatry* 8 (1973): 131.
30. Grof et al., "LSD-Assisted Psychotherapy," 131.
31. Grof et al., "LSD-Assisted Psychotherapy," 132.
32. Grof et al., "LSD-Assisted Psychotherapy," 133.
33. Grof et al., "LSD-Assisted Psychotherapy," 135.
34. Grof et al., "LSD-Assisted Psychotherapy," 143.
35. Grof et al., "LSD-Assisted Psychotherapy," 143.
36. Charles S. Grob, "The Use of Psilocybin in Patients with Advanced Cancer and Existential Anxiety," in *Psychedelic Medicine: New Evidence for Hallucinogenic Substances as Treatments*, ed. M. Winkelman and T. B. Roberts (Westport, CT: Praeger, 2007), 214.

37. Grob, "The Use of Psilocybin," 208.
38. Grob, "The Use of Psilocybin," 212.
39. Charles S. Grob et al., "Pilot Study of Psilocybin Treatment for Anxiety in Patients with Advanced-Stage Cancer," *Archives of General Psychiatry* 68 (2011): 78.
40. Grob, "The Use of Psilocybin," 208–209.
41. Grob, "The Use of Psilocybin," 213.
42. Grob, "The Use of Psilocybin," 211.
43. Grob et al., "Pilot Study," 1.
44. Alexander Zaitchik, "Flashback! Psychedelic Research Returns," *Salon*, September 28, 2011. https://www.salon.com/2011/09/28/the_new_lsd_cure/.
45. Jennifer Bleyer, "Once Taboo, Psychedelics Are Making an Enlightening Medical Comeback," *NYU Alumni Magazine*, Spring 2013. Nyu.edu/alumni.magazine/issue 20.
46. Bleyer, "Once Taboo," 5.
47. Alex Liu, "Psychedelic Therapy: New Research Shows Psychedelics Might Hold Therapeutic Potential for Those Dealing with Death," *ScienceLine*, February 24, 2010. scienceline.org/2010/02/psychedelic-therapy.
48. Liu, "Psychedelic Therapy."
49. Zaitchik, "Flashback!"
50. Jeffrey Kripal, *Esalen: America and the Religion of No Religion* (Chicago: University of Chicago Press, 2007), 226.
51. Glausser, *Cultural Encyclopedia*, 44.
52. Fisher, "Psychotherapy for the Dying," 12.
53. Fisher, "Psychotherapy for the Dying," 12.
54. Fisher, "Psychotherapy for the Dying," 14.
55. Fisher, "Psychotherapy for the Dying," 14.
56. Fisher, "Psychotherapy for the Dying," 15.

BIBLIOGRAPHY

Abrams, M. H., E. Talbot Donaldson, Hallett Smith, Robert M. Adams, Samuel Holt Monk, George H. Ford, and David Daiches, eds. *The Norton Anthology of English Literature*. 2 vols. New York: W. W. Norton and Co., 1962.

Abrams, M. H., E. Talbot Donaldson, Hallett Smith, Robert M. Adams, Samuel Holt Monk, George H. Ford, and David Daiches, eds. *The Norton Anthology of English Literature*. 2nd ed. 2 vols. New York: W. W. Norton and Co., 1968.

Abrams, M. H., E. Talbot Donaldson, Hallett Smith, Robert M. Adams, Samuel Holt Monk, George H. Ford, and David Daiches, eds. *The Norton Anthology of English Literature*. 3rd ed. 2 vols. New York: W. W. Norton and Co., 1974.

Abrams, M. H., E. Talbot Donaldson, Hallett Smith, Robert M. Adams, Samuel Holt Monk, George H. Ford, and David Daiches, eds. *The Norton Anthology of English Literature*. 4th ed. 2 vols. New York: W. W. Norton and Co., 1979.

Abrams, M. H., E. Talbot Donaldson, Hallett Smith, Robert M. Adams, Samuel Holt Monk, George H. Ford, David Daiches, eds. *The Norton Anthology of English Literature*. 5th ed. 2 vols. New York: W. W. Norton and Co., 1986.

Abrams, M. H., E. Talbot Donaldson, Hallett Smith, Robert M. Adams, Samuel Holt Monk, George H. Ford, David Daiches, eds. *The Norton Anthology of English Literature*. 6th ed. 2 vols. New York: W. W. Norton and Co., 1993.

Abrams, M. H., Stephen Greenblatt, Alfred David, George M. Logan, Barbara K. Lewalski, Lawrence Lipking, Jack Stillinter, eds. *The Norton Anthology of English Literature*. 7th ed. 2 vols. New York: W. W. Norton and Co., 2000.

Aczel, Amir. *Why Science Does Not Disprove God*. New York: William Morrow, 2014.

Alvarez, David P. "Reason and Religious Tolerance: Mary Astell's Critique of Shaftesbury." *Eighteenth-Century Studies* 44 (2011): 475–494.

American Family Association. "The Naughty-or-Nice 2016 Retailer List." Afa.net. November 30, 2016. www.afa.net/who-we-are/press-releases/2016/11/whos-naughty-who-s-nice/.

American Psychiatric Association. *Diagnostic and Statistical Manual of Mental Disorders*. 5th ed. Arlington, VA: American Psychiatric Publishing, 2013.

Anderson, David E. "The Grandeur of God and the Life of the Poet." *Religion and Ethics Newsweekly*, March 20, 2009. Pbs.org/wnet/religionandethics.

Aquinas, Thomas. *Summa Theologica*. Translated by Fathers of the English Dominican Province. 3 vols. New York: Benziger Brothers, 1947.

Ariely, Dan, and Aline Gruneisen. "The Price of Greed." *Scientific American Mind* 24 (2013): 38–42.

Asad, Talal. *Formations of the Secular: Christianity, Islam, Modernism*. Stanford, CA: Stanford University Press, 2003.

Associated Press. "Pope Francis Praises Turin Shroud as an 'Icon of Love.'" *Guardian*, June 21, 2015.

Berlinerblau, Jacques. "The Crisis in Secular Studies." *Chronicle of Higher Education*, chronicle.com, September 8, 2014. www.chronicle.com/article/The-Crisis-in-Secular-Studies/148599.

Blair, Leonardo. "Man in Pope Francis Exorcism Story Says He's Still Possessed by Demons." *Christian Post Reporter*, May 31, 2013.

Bleyer, Jennifer. "Once Taboo, Psychedelics Are Making an Enlightening Medical Comeback." *NYU Alumni Magazine*. Nyu.edu/alumni.magazine/issue 20, Spring 2013.

"Blood of St. Januarius Liquefies during Francis's Visit to Naples." Catholic Herald, March 21, 2015. www.catholicherald.co.uk > Latest News.

Bloom, Harold. *A Map of Misreading*. New York: Oxford University Press, 1975.

Brown, Candy Gunther. *Testing Prayer: Science and Healing*. Cambridge, MA: Harvard University Press, 2012.

Cacioppo, Stephanie, and John T. Cacioppo. "Lust for Life." *Scientific Amerian Mind* 24 (2013): 56–63.

Calvin, John. *The Institutes of the Christian Religion*. Translated by Henry Beveridge. Grand Rapids, MI: Christian Classics Ethereal Library, 2002.

Collins, Francis. *The Language of God: A Scientist Presents Evidence for Belief*. New York: Free Press, 2006.

Conner, Claire. *Wrapped in the Flag: A Personal History of America's Radical Right*. Boston: Beacon Press, 2013.

Coruh, Basak, Hana Ayele, Meredith Pugh, and Thomas Mulligan. "Does Religious Activity Improve Health Outcomes? A Critical Review of the Recent Literature." *Explore* 1 (2005): 180–191.

Crusius, Jan, and Thomas Mussweiler. "Untangling Envy." *Scientific American Mind* 24 (2013): 34–37.

Damrosch, David. "The Mirror and the Window: Reflections on Anthology Construction." *Pedagogy* 1 (2001): 207–214.

Damrosch, David, Christopher Baswell, Clare Carroll, Kevin J. H. Dettmar, Heather Henderson, Constance Jordan, Peter J. Manning, et al., eds. *The Longman Anthology of British Literature*. 2 vols. New York: Longman, 1999.

Davies, Brian. *The Thought of Thomas Aquinas*. Oxford: Oxford University Press, 1993.

Dawkins, Richard. *The God Delusion*. Boston: Houghton Mifflin, 2006.

De Botton, Alain. *Religion for Atheists: A Non-Believer's Guide to the Uses of Religion*. New York: Vintage, 2012.

Delbanco, Andrew. *The Death of Satan: How Americans Have Lost the Sense of Evil*. New York: Farrar, Strauss, and Giroux, 1995.

Dennett, Daniel C. *Breaking the Spell: Religion as a Natural Phenomenon*. New York: Penguin, 2006.

Denvir, Daniel. "A Short History of the War on Christmas: How Everyone from Bill O'Reilly to Jon Stewart Became a Co-Conspirator in an Annual Farce." *Politico*, December 16, 2013. www.politico.com/magazine/story/2013/12/war-on-christmas-short-history.

Diamond, Stephen A. "Exorcism as Psychotherapy: A Clinical Psychologist Examines So-Called Demonic Possession." *Psychology Today*, February 5, 2011. https://www.psychologytoday.com/.../exorcism-psychotherapy-clinical-psychologist.

Doblin, Rick. "Pahnke's 'Good Friday Experiment': A Long-Term Follow-Up and Methodological Critique." *Journal of Transpersonal Psychology* 23 (1991): 1–28.

Donnelly, Nick. "Pope Francis Challenges Priests Who Don't Believe in the Devil or the Power of Exorcism." *Protect the Pope* (blog). October 13, 2013. protectthepope.com/?p=8672.

Donoghue, Denis. "The Flight of Gerard Manley Hopkins." *New York Review of Books*, July 18, 1991, 14–18.

Feinberg, Cara. "The Placebo Phenomenon." *Harvard Magazine*, January/February 2013, 11–14.

Fessenden, Tracy. *Culture and Redemption: Religion, the Secular, and American Literature*. Princeton, NJ: Princeton University Press, 2006.

Feuerstein, Joshua. Facebook page. November 5, 2015. https://www.facebook.com/joshua.feuerstein.

Finkel, Eli J., and Caitlin W. Duffy. "The Thin Line between Love and Wrath." *Scientific American Mind* 24 (2013): 50–55.

Fisher, Gary. "Psychotherapy for the Dying: Principles and Illustrative Cases with Special Reference to the Use of LSD." *Omega* 1 (1970): 3–16.

Gallagher, Richard. "As a Psychiatrist, I Diagnose Mental Illness. Also, I Help Spot Demonic Possession." *Washington Post*, July 1, 2016.

Ghose, Tia. "Is It a Fake? DNA Testing Deepens Mystery of Shroud of Turin." *Live Science*, October 23, 2015. https://www.livescience.com > Strange News.

Gingerich, Owen. *God's Universe*. Cambridge, MA: Harvard University Press, 2006.

Glausser, Wayne. *Cultural Encyclopedia of LSD*. Jefferson, NC: McFarland, 2011.

Gould, Stephen Jay. *Rocks of Ages: Science and Religion in the Fullness of Life.* New York: Ballantine, 1999.

Greenblatt, Stephen, Carol T. Christ, Alfred David, Barbara K. Lewalski, Lawrence Lipking, George M. Logan, Deidre Shauna Lynch, et al., eds. *The Norton Anthology of English Literature.* 8th ed. 2 vols. New York: W. W. Norton and Co., 2006.

Greenblatt, Stephen, Carol T. Christ, Alfred David, Barbara K. Lewalski, Lawrence Lipking, George M. Logan, Deidre Shauna Lynch, et al., eds. *The Norton Anthology of English Literature.* 9th ed. 2 vols. New York: W. W. Norton and Co., 2012.

Greene, Joshua D. "The Secret Joke of Kant's Soul." In *Moral Psychology,* Vol. 3, *The Neuroscience of Morality: Emotion, Brain Disorders, and Development,* edited by Walter Sinnott-Armstrong, 35–80. Cambridge, MA: MIT Press, 2008.

Griffiths, R. R., W. A. Richards, U. McCann, and R. Jesse. "Psilocybin Can Occasion Mystical-Type Experiences Having Substantial and Sustained Personal Meaning and Significance." *Psychopharmacology* 187 (2006): 268–283.

Grob, Charles S. "The Use of Psilocybin in Patients with Advanced Cancer and Existential Anxiety." In *Psychedelic Medicine: New Evidence for Hallucinogenic Substances as Treatments,* edited by M. Winkelman and T. B. Roberts, 205–216. Westport, CT: Praeger, 2007.

Grob, Charles S., A. L. Danforth, G. S. Chopra, M. Hagerty, C. R. McKay, A. L. Halberstadt, and G. R. Greer. "Pilot Study of Psilocybin Treatment for Anxiety in Patients with Advanced-Stage Cancer." *Archives of General Psychiatry* 68 (2011): 71–78.

Grof, S., L. E. Goodman, W. A. Richards, and A. A. Kurland. "LSD-Assisted Psychotherapy in Patients with Terminal Cancer." *International Pharmacopsychiatry* 8 (1973): 129–144.

Harris, Sam. *The End of Faith: Religion, Terror, and the Future of Reason.* New York: Norton, 2004.

Hawking, Stephen. *A Brief History of Time.* New York: Bantam, 1988.

Herbst, Winfrid. *Call the Priest.* St. Louis: Queen's Work, 1952. https://www.ecatholic2000.com/cts/untitled-66.shtml.

Hitchens, Christopher. *God Is Not Great: How Religion Poisons Everything.* New York: Twelve Books, 2007.

Holt, Jim. *Why Does the World Exist? An Existential Detective Story.* New York: Liveright, 2012.

Holyoake, George Jacob. *English Secularism: A Confession of Belief.* 1896. Project Gutenberg, 2011. http://www.gutenberg.org/ebooks/38104.

Huxley, Aldous. *The Doors of Perception.* New York: Harper and Brothers, 1954.

Ivereigh, Austen. *The Great Reformer: Francis and the Making of a Radical Pope.* New York: Picador, 2014.

Jammer, Max. *Einstein and Religion.* Princeton, NJ: Princeton University Press, 1999.

Jayawickreme, Eranda, and William Fleeson. "Does Whole Trait Theory Work for the Virtues?" In *Moral Psychology*, Vol. 5. *Virtue and Character*, edited by Walter Sinnott-Armstrong and Christian B. Miller, 75–103. Cambridge, MA: MIT Press, 2017.

Jones, Terry. *Chaucer's Knight: The Portrait of a Medieval Mercenary*. London: Methuen, 1980.

Kast, Eric. "LSD and the Dying Patient." *The Chicago Medical School Quarterly* 26 (1966): 80–87.

Kermode, Frank, John Hollander, Harold Bloom, Lionel Trilling, and Martin Price, eds. *The Oxford Anthology of English Literature*. 2 vols. New York: Oxford University Press, 1973.

Krauss, Lawrence M. *A Universe from Nothing: Why There Is Something Rather Than Nothing*. New York: Atria, 2012.

Kripal, Jeffrey. *Esalen: America and the Religion of No Religion*. Chicago: University of Chicago Press, 2007.

Kristjansson, Kristjan. "A Tale of Two Default Approaches: Some Old Answers for a New Theory." In *Moral Psychology*, Vol. 5. *Virtue and Character*, edited by Walter Sinnott-Armstrong and Christian B. Miller, 587–595. Cambridge, MA: MIT Press, 2017.

Leary, Timothy, Ralph Metzner, and Richard Alpert. *The Psychedelic Experience: A Manual Based on the Tibetan Book of the Dead*. New York: Citadel, 1964.

Leithauser, Brad. "A Passionate Clamor." *New York Review of Books*, April 14, 2004, 45–48.

Lewis, C. S. *The Screwtape Letters*. 1942. Reprint, New York: HarperOne, 2015.

Leyshon, Gareth. "Exorcism and Prayers for Deliverance: A Historical Review of the Developments since the Late Nineteenth Century." June 28, 2016. www.drgareth.info/Deliverance-X.pdf.

Lightman, Alan. *The Accidental Universe: The World You Thought You Knew*. New York: Vintage, 2013.

Liu, Alex. "Psychedelic Therapy: New Research Shows Psychedelics Might Hold Therapeutic Potential for Those Dealing with Death." *ScienceLine*, February 24, 2010. scienceline.org/2010/02/psychedelic-therapy.

Liuzza, Roy, Joseph Black, Leonard Conolly, Kate Flint, Isobel Grundy, Jerome McGann, Anne Prescott, Barry Qualls, and Claire Waters, eds. *The Broadview Anthology of British Literature*. 6 vols. Peterborough, ON: Broadview Press, 2006.

Maher, Bill. *Religulous*. Directed by Larry Charles. Los Angeles: Lions Gate, 2008. DVD.

Marshall, Taylor. "Pope Francis and Popular Devotions." *Taylor Marshall PhD* (blog), May 12, 2014. taylormarshall.com/screen-shot-2014-05-12-at-10-37-02-am.

Martin, Robert. *Gerard Manley Hopkins: A Very Private Life*. London: Faber and Faber, 2011.

Matyszczyk, Chris. "Stephen Hawking Makes It Clear: There Is No God." CNET. September 26, 2014. https://www.cnet.com/news/stephen-hawking-makes-it-clear-there-is-no-god.

McInerny, Ralph. *Ethica Thomistica*. Washington, DC: Catholic University of America Press, 1997.

McInerny, Ralph, and John O'Callaghan. "Saint Thomas Aquinas." In *Stanford Encyclopedia of Philosophy*. Stanford University, 1997. Article published July 12, 1999. Revised May 23, 2014. https://plato.stanford.edu/entries/aquinas.

Menand, Louis. "Saved from Drowning: Barthelme Reconsidered." *New Yorker*, Februrary 23, 2009, 68–76.

Milton, John. *Paradise Lost*. In *John Milton: Complete Poems and Major Prose*, edited by Merritt Y. Hughes. Indianapolis: Odyssey, 1957.

Montgomery, Peter. "Religious Right's Annual War on the 'War on Christmas' Has a New Field Marshal." *Right Wing Watch*, November 17, 2016. www.rightwingwatch.org/.../religious-rights-annual-war-on-the-war-on-christmas-has-a-new-field-marshal.

Mortenson, Terry. "Young Earth Creationist View Summarized and Defended." *Answers in Genesis*, February 16, 2011. https://answersingenesis.org/.../young-earth/young-earth-creationist-view-summarized-and-defended.

Niebuhr, Gustav. "Is Satan Real? Most People Think Not." *New York Times*, May 10, 1997.

Nixon, J. Peter. "Has Hell Frozen Over?" *U.S. Catholic*, November 15, 2011, 12–17.

Oxford English Dictionary (OED). 2nd ed. 20 vols. Oxford: Oxford University Press, 1989.

Peacham, Henry. *The Garden of Eloquence*. 1593. Reprint, Gainesville, FL: Scholars' Facsimiles and Reprints, 1954.

Pew Research Center. "Quotes on Stem Cell Research." July 17, 2008. http://www.pewforum.org/2008/07/17/quotes-on-stem-cell-research-from-political-religious-and-other-prominent-figures.

Pew Research Center. "Religious Groups' Official Positions on Stem Cell Research." July 17, 2008. www.pewforum.org/2008/.../religious-groups-official-positions-on-stem-cell-research.

Polkinghorne, John. *Science and Religion in Quest of Truth*. New Haven, CT: Yale University Press, 2011.

Prose, Francine. *Gluttony*. New York: Oxford University Press, 2003.

"Putting the Placebo Effect to Work." *Harvard Health Letter*, April 2012. https://www.health.harvard.edu/mind-and-mood/putting-the-placebo-effect-to-work.

Ribuffo, Leo P. "Henry Ford and 'The International Jew.'" *American Jewish History* 69 (1980): 437–477.

Rini, Regina A. "Morality and Cognitive Science." In *Internet Encyclopedia of Philosophy*, June 30, 2015. www.iep.utm.edu/m-cog-sci.

Roberts, L., I. Ahmed, and A. Davison. "Intercessory Prayer for the Alleviation of Ill Health." *Cochrane Database of Systematic Reviews*, 2009. www.cochrane.org/.../SCHIZ_intercessory-prayer-for-the-alleviation-of-ill-health.

Rosica, Thomas. "Why Is Pope Francis So Obsessed with the Devil?" CNN.com. July 20, 2015. www.cnn.com/2015/07/20/living/pope-francis-devil/index.html.

Rushdie, Salman. *The Satanic Verses*. New York: Viking, 1988.

Sherry, Richard, and Desiderius Erasmus. *A Treatise of Schemes and Tropes: and His Translations of the Education of Children by Desiderius Erasmus*, 1550. Gainesville, FL: Scholars' Facsimiles and Reprints, 1961.

Shesgreen, Sean. "Canonizing the Canonizer: A Short History of *The Norton Anthology of English Literature*." *Critical Inquiry* 35 (2009): 293–318.

Simring, Karen Schrock. "Accidental Gluttons." *Scientific American Mind* 24 (2013): 26–33.

Smith, John. *The Mystery of Rhetoric Unveil'd*. London: Robert Clavel, 1688. Early English Books online. https://quod.lib.umich.edu/e/eebo/A59234.0001.001.

Spinoza, Baruch. *The Ethics and Selected Letters*. Translated by Samuel Shirley. Indianapolis: Hackett, 1982.

Stanford, Peter. "Exorcism: What Does the Boom in Demand Tell Us about Pope Francis' Catholic Church?" *Independent*, April 14, 2015.

Stewart, William C., M. P. Adams, J. A. Stewart, and L. A. Nelson. "Review of Clinical Medicine and Religious Practice." *Journal of Religion and Health* 52 (2013): 91–106.

Squires, Nick. "Pope Francis Links Turin Shroud to Jesus Christ." Telegraph. co.uk, March 30, 2013. http://www.telegraph.co.uk/news/religion/9962709/Pope-Francis-links-Turin-Shroud-to-Jesus-Christ.

Taylor, Charles. *A Secular Age*. Cambridge, MA: Harvard University Press, 2007.

Thurston, Herbert. "Relics." In *The Catholic Encyclopedia*, edited by Charles G. Herbermann, Edward A. Pace, Conde B. Pallen, Thomas J. Shahan, and John J. Wynne. New York: Robert Appleton Company, 1910. Accessed in New Advent, November 6, 2016. http://www.newadvent.org/cathen/08295a.htm.

Thurston, Herbert. "St. Januarius." In *The Catholic Encyclopedia*, edited by Charles G. Herbermann, Edward A. Pace, Conde B. Pallen, Thomas J. Shahan, and John J. Wynne. New York: Robert Appleton Company, 1910. Accessed in New Advent. http://www.newadvent.org/cathen/08295a.htm.

Tiberius, Valerie. "Does Virtue Make Us Happy? A New Theory for an Old Question." In *Moral Psychology*, Vol. 5: *Virtue and Character*, edited by Walter Sinnott-Armstrong and Christian B. Miller, 547–577. Cambridge, MA: MIT Press, 2017.

Toner, Patrick. "Extreme Unction." In *The Catholic Encyclopedia*, edited by Charles G. Herbermann, Edward A. Pace, Conde B. Pallen, Thomas J. Shahan, and

John J. Wynne. New York: Robert Appleton Company, 1910. Accessed in New Advent. http://www.newadvent.org/cathen/05716a.htm.

Tracy, Jessica L. "Pride and Power." *Scientific American Mind* 24 (2013): 64–68.

United States Conference of Catholic Bishops. "Popular Devotional Practices: Basic Questions and Answers." November 12, 2003. www.usccb.org > Prayer and Worship > Prayers and Devotions > Prayers.

Upson, Sandra. "Prodding our Inner Sloth." *Scientific American Mind* 24 (2013): 44–49.

Vallely, Paul. *Pope Francis: The Struggle for the Soul of Catholicism.* New York: Bloomsbury, 2015.

Viviano, Frank. "Why Shroud of Turin's Secrets Continue to Elude Science." *National Geographic*, April 17, 2015. http://news.nationalgeographic.com/2015/04/150417-shroud-turin-relics-jesus-catholic-church-religion-science/.

Warner, Michael, Jonathan VanAntwerpen, and Craig Calhoun, eds. *Varieties of Secularism in a Secular Age.* Cambridge, MA: Harvard University Press, 2010.

Weinberg, Steven. "A Designer Universe." *New York Review of Books*, October 21, 1999, 46–48.

Weinberg, Steven. *The First Three Minutes: A Modern View of the Origin of the Universe.* Glasgow: William Collins, 1977.

Wooden, Cindy. "Battle with the Devil: Pope Francis Frames the Fight in Jesuit Terms." *National Catholic Reporter*, April 18, 2013.

Wyatt, Caroline. "Pope Francis's Reforms Polarise the Vatican." BBC.com. March 27. 2016. www.bbc.com/news/world-europe-35869656.

Zaitchik, Alexander. "Flashback! Psychedelic Research Returns." *Salon*, September 28, 2011. https://www.salon.com/2011/09/28/the_new_lsd_cure/.

INDEX

Abrams, M. H., 72–74, 91–92
acedia (lack of care), xi, 125
Act of Contrition prayer, 127
Aczel, Amir, 49
Adams, Douglas, 39
Adams, Robert: on Locke and Christianity, 81; on Satan in Milton's *Paradise Lost*, 72, 75, 77–81
Agnes of Montepulciano (Catholic saint), 35–36
agnosticism, 7, 33
Alexandria, siege (1365) of, 82
Ali, Muhammad, 148
Alpert, Richard, 155–56
Al-Qaeda, 87
Alvarez, David, 76
Amorth, Gabriele, 111
Anderson, David E., 90
anointing of the sick. *See* extreme unction
anorgasmia, 133
antifoundationalism, 76
anti-Semitism, 10, 83
anxiety: end of life and, xi, 25, 163, 167–68; extreme unction and, 155; greed and, 143–44; procrastination and, 127; psychedelic drugs and therapy for, ix, 25, 150, 155, 157, 163, 167–68
apodioxis, 34–35

apophrades ("ratio of revision"), 46–47
aporia: definition of, 26; new atheists on the universe's origins and, 26–30, 38, 42, 47–48; poststructuralism and, 26–27
Appleby, R. Scott, 111
Aquinas, Thomas: Aristotle and, 25, 120–22, 125–27, 132, 139–40, 146; Augustine and, 130, 132; charity and, 140; the deadly sins and, 24–25, 119–20, 124, 135; envy and, 138–41; ethics and, 120–22; *eudaimonia* (flourishing) and, 121; gluttony and, 129–32; greed and, 142–44; is-ought problem and, 123; Jerome and, 139; lust and, 132–35; pride and, 145–48; pusillanimity and, 146; reasoning and, 122–23, 129; revenge and, 135–36, 138; sloth and, 125–28; usury and, 142; wrath and, 135–38; zeal and, 139
Ariely, Dan, 143–44
Aristotle: Aquinas and, 25, 120–22, 125–27, 132, 139–40, 146; contemporary cognitive science and, 120–22; envy and, 139–40; ethics and, 120–22; *eudaimonia* (flourishing) and, 121; is-ought problem and, 123; lust and, 132; pusillanimity and, 146; reasoning and, 121–23, 125; sloth and, 125–27; virtuous moderation and, 121, 129; wrath and, 136; zeal and, 139

Einstein, Albert: atheism and, 57, 59–60; deism and, 58, 61; faithful scientists' citation of, 56–59, 62–63; on God and the origins of the universe, 53; on his own sense of religious belief, 59; on the mysterious, 56; pantheism and, 61; on quantum mechanics, 58, 65; on relationship between science and religion, 58; on science and spirituality, 59–60; Spinoza and, xi, 60, 62
Einstein and Religion (Jammer), 58–60
Eliot, T. S., 83
Elizabeth II (queen of England), 87
embryonic stem cell research: bioethicists' interpretation of, 15–16; blastocysts and, 15–16; fertility treatment embryos and, 13–14, 16; religious opponents of, 13–15, 17–18; therapeutic potential of, 12–13, 17–18
The End of Faith (Harris), 27, 39, 44
envy: Aquinas on, 138–41; Aristotle on, 139–40; charity and, 140; contemporary opinions regarding, 125; definition of, 139; desired end of, 135, 138, 141; emulation of virtue as possible response to, 139; evolutionary aspects of, 140–41; Gregory I on, 135, 138; Jerome and, 139; pride and, 147; *Scientific American* essay on, 124, 140–41; zeal and, 139–40
Epicurus, 35
Episcopalianism, 14
Ethica Thomistica (McInerny), 120
Ethics (Spinoza), 60
eudaimonia (flourishing), 121
Evagrius Ponticus, 138
Evangelicals, 14
Eve (Book of Genesis), 78, 80
evolution: Catholicism and, 99; creationism's rejection of, 3–4; Dawkins on, 31; development of religious behaviors and, 168; envy and, 140–41; faithful scientists and, 66–68; genetic mutation and, 66–68; natural selection and, 31, 53
exorcism, 110–11, 113–14, 117

extreme unction: Buddhist rituals compared to, 156; cancer patients and, 152; confession and, 153–54, 159; consciousness and, 154; Council of Trent on, 152, 155; criterion for administering, 151–52, 170; Epistle of James and, 149–50; grace and, 152–53, 155; healing of the body and, 152, 159; healing of the soul and, 155, 166; Holy Spirit and, 149–50; mortal sin as reason to deny, 170; placebo effect and, 153; Protestant views of, 149–50, 152, 159; psychedelic drugs and therapy compared to, ix, 25, 150–52, 154, 159, 164, 171; remission of sins and, 153–54; salvation and, 149, 152–53

The Faerie Queene (Spenser), 24, 71, 75, 83–85
faithful scientists: appeals to authority by, 56–59, 61–63; atheism challenged by, 49–50, 58; evolution and, 66–68; fideistic certainties and, 52–54; "God of the gaps" problem and, 66; infelicitous mix of scientific and religious discourses among, 63–67; intercessory prayer and, 108; Non-Overlapping Magisteria and, 7, 49–50; pathopoeia employed by, 68–70; Romantic diction and, 54–56; scientific materialism and, 49; theodicy as a challenge for, 67–70
Fessenden, Tracy, 22
Feuerstein, Joshua, 11
"final theory" (physics), 47–48
Finkel, Eli J., 136–38
First Amendment, 11
Fisher, Gary, 161–64, 170–71
Fleeson, William, 122
Flourish (Seligman), 122
Ford, George, 88–89
Ford, Henry, 10
Foster, Reginald, 5–6
Foucault, Michel, 18
Francis (pope). *See also* Bergoglio, Jorge: on atheism, 95; capitalism's excesses criticized by, 95, 102, 105; exorcism and, 113–14, 117; on global warming and